AGE O
AGE O

Edgar Cayce's first psychic pronouncements made headlines in the *New York Times* and stirred debate among doctors and scientists. In following years thousands flocked to him and sent him letters asking for help. In this work an acclaimed writer goes back to the roots of the Cayce phenomenon to reveal The Sleeping Prophet's answers to 10 fundamental questions of life, including:

- **How his guide to diet has become a medically proven part of total good health.**
- **How his concept of the unconscious mind can be linked to Freud's—and has helped thousands become more productive and more loving in their lives.**
- **How his view of hostility, its causes and results, is an important aspect of stress-reduction today.**
- **How the search for absolute religious truth can reveal a common ground for us all.**

John G. Fuller is a veteran documentary film producer and bestselling author whose work has taken him around the world. In this thoughtful and insightful book he examines Edgar Cayce's psychic history, his method and his concepts—for a striking profile of the teachings that opened the door to a new age.

☆

Books in The Edgar Cayce Series

DREAMS: YOUR MAGIC MIRROR
EDGAR CAYCE ON DIET AND HEALTH
EDGAR CAYCE ON HEALING
EDGAR CAYCE ON RELIGION AND
PSYCHIC EXPERIENCE
EDGAR CAYCE ON ESP
EDGAR CAYCE ON ATLANTIS
THE EDGAR CAYCE READER: VOLS. 1 AND 2
EDGAR CAYCE ON DREAMS
EDGAR CAYCE ON PROPHECY
EDGAR CAYCE ON REINCARNATION
EDGAR CAYCE ON JESUS AND HIS CHURCH
EDGAR CAYCE ON THE DEAD SEA SCROLLS
EDGAR CAYCE ENCYCLOPEDIA OF HEALING
EDGAR CAYCE ON MYSTERIES OF THE MIND
EDGAR CAYCE ON SECRETS OF THE UNIVERSE AND
HOW TO USE THEM IN YOUR LIFE
EDGAR CAYCE ANSWERS LIFE'S
10 MOST IMPORTANT QUESTIONS
EDGAR CAYCE ON CHANNELING YOUR HIGHER SELF
YOU CAN REMEMBER YOUR PAST LIVES

Published by
WARNER BOOKS

EDGAR CAYCE

ANSWERS LIFE'S 10 MOST IMPORTANT QUESTIONS

BY JOHN G. FULLER
UNDER THE EDITORSHIP OF
CHARLES THOMAS CAYCE

WARNER BOOKS

A Warner Communications Company

WARNER BOOKS EDITION

Cover design by Karen Katz

Warner Books, Inc.
666 Fifth Avenue
New York, N.Y. 10103

 A Warner Communications Company

Printed in the United States of America

First Printing: June, 1989

10 9 8 7 6 5 4 3 2 1

ACKNOWLEDGMENTS

There couldn't be a better expression of Edgar Cayce's ideal of selfless service to others than is found in the staff of the A.R.E., especially when an outsider, as I am, looks for help in putting together a book like this.

A.R.E. president Charles Thomas Cayce not only offered his assistance far beyond the line of duty, but encouraged many staffers to provide great help. Some are mentioned in the text of this book. Others include such stalwart Cayce students as Keith VonderOhe, Bob Smith, Chris Fazel, Jeanette Thomas, Marie Allen, and especially Bob Jeffries.

The intellectual labor of outside editor Ed Sedarbaum deserves hefty additional thanks via this inadequate method of acknowledgment.

CONTENTS

Foreword *by Charles Thomas Cayce*   1
Introduction   23
Question 1:   Is There a God?   31
Question 2:   What Is the Real Purpose of
My Life?   69
Question 3:   How Can I Find Peace in
a Turbulent World?   89
Question 4:   How Can I Acquire My Best
Health and Highest Energies?   105
Question 5:   How Can I Work and Love at
My Highest Capacities?   129
Question 6:   How Can I Get Rid of Frustrations,
Hostility, and Negative Attitudes?   159
Question 7:   How Can I Overcome Feelings of
Guilt and Fear?   179
Question 8:   How Can We Know the Will of God
and the Nature of Free Will?   193
Question 9:   Is There Life after Death?   207
Question 10:   What Religion Reveals the
Greatest Truth?   227
Epilogue: Impact on the Author   235
The A.R.E. Today   245

FOREWORD

A Brief Look at the Life and Work of Edgar Cayce

The past few years have seen an increased public interest in altered states of consciousness, intuition, and psychic ability and a wider circulation of information about these topics. As part of the growing awareness about individuals who have had unusual powers of perception, the name Edgar Cayce has become more and more well known. Literally millions of copies of books about his life and work have been sold. Many books that are not specifically about Edgar Cayce include sections on him, and several widely viewed television programs have mentioned his name.

It's safe to say that a very large number of people have come to hear of Edgar Cayce. And yet, many of these people—perhaps the great majority—have only a vague idea of who he was, what he did, and the kind of information that came through him in his psychic readings. Some who are just barely acquainted with Edgar Cayce might feel a certain curiosity about the man; at times, they might find themselves wondering whether there was any value in what he said and did.

Edgar Cayce Answers Life's 10 Most Important Questions is written primarily for such people. People with questions about Edgar Cayce and the content of the psychic discourses, known as readings, that he gave. People who are curious, perhaps skeptical. Those who are not necessarily willing to commit themselves to belief in unusual events of this sort, but who want to know more about them. Those who are at least willing to consider the question, Is there something worthwhile here?

The purpose of this book is to provide for these people an introduction to Edgar Cayce—my grandfather—and some of the concepts that were received through him. The aim is to present in a simple, clear way some of the basic ideas and philosophical themes given in the Cayce material, without assuming that the reader has any prior knowledge about Edgar Cayce and the kind of material he transmitted.

This type of introductory volume calls for an author whose attitude toward the material and whose familiarity with it roughly match that of the intended readers. The person best suited for the job will be someone who is open to the possibility that valid information can be received through nonphysical means, but not necessarily convinced of it.

Our ideal author will not be a person who has spent a lifetime writing about unusual phenomena and nothing else; rather, he or she will have worked in several diverse fields and will have given unbiased accounts of many different aspects of human experience. The job requires someone able to reach a wide spectrum of readers, give them an unslanted description of the material, and let them decide for themselves whether to pursue their initial interest further. The person should be curious, objective, and maybe a bit skeptical in some areas—in other words, a reporter rather than a salesman or a total believer.

John G. Fuller's background suits him to this task admirably. He has produced popular and highly acclaimed documentary work in a variety of areas. Space vehicles, the oceans, rescue squads, forestry, inner-city Neighborhood Youth Corps, irrigation projects, drug abuse, tornadoes and other natural disasters—John has reported on all these subjects and more, creating accurate and evocative images both in words and on film.

For over ten years John was a columnist for *Saturday Review,* and he has contributed to *Reader's Digest, Omni, Ladies' Home Journal, Science Digest, Look,* and *Playboy* magazines. He has authored a number of books, including the best-sellers *The Interrupted Journey* and *Incident at Exeter*. His written work has been honored by the American Library Association, the New York Academy of Sciences, and the National Association of Teachers.

John has produced the Emmy-winning Public Television show *The Great American Dream Machine*. Among his other credits are over seventy-five documentary and educational films and television programs, including *Light Across the Shadow,* winner of the Sigma Delta Chi Journalism Award as best documentary of 1965, and *Century III: The Oceans,* which was honored at the Belgrade Film Festival of 1977 and received the Golden Eagle Ciné Award. He has written, produced, and/or directed presentations for all three major television net-

works, his work having been seen on CBS's *The Twentieth Century* and NBC's *Dupont Show of the Week*.

In addition to his vast experience and his ability as a
reporter, John possesses another quality important to
anyone seeking to write about unusual human powers:
courage. In some quarters, anyone who's even inclined
to investigate such phenomena is immediately suspect,
his credibility open to question. John has been willing to
take this risk. Several of his books have provided accurate descriptions of extraordinary human experiences.

For example, in the widely read *Arigo: Surgeon of the
Rusty Knife,* John recorded the story of a Brazilian man
who went into trance and, supposedly with discarnate
surgeons working through him, performed complicated
operations on large numbers of people in a nonsterile
environment, achieving remarkable results. John not only
took on this unconventional assignment, he succeeded in
getting his account published by *Reader's Digest,* in spite
of that magazine's long-standing policy of avoiding material dealing with such unusual subjects. This in itself
testifies to his accuracy, thoroughness, and objectivity.

I first met John Fuller about five years ago. At the
time he was involved in a writing project examining
technological advancements that might provide evidence
of life after death. John visited us here at the Association
for Research and Enlightenment, the organization established to study the Edgar Cayce material, and we talked
for a while about my grandfather's work.

When I asked John if he would be interested in writing
something about Edgar Cayce, he came up with the idea
of examining what Edgar Cayce had said about some of
the basic questions in life that confront all of us. This

would give him a chance to do some exploring in an area that interested him, and he could then present his findings to others who, like John himself, had heard of Edgar Cayce and wanted to discover more about him, but were not particularly knowledgeable about the man and his work. The idea seemed like a good one to me.

A little while later, one of the publishers at Warner Books got in touch with me. Some years ago, Warner had produced one of the first series of books for general readership based on concepts from the Cayce readings. Now, in response to the increasing public interest in the area of uncommon human abilities, they were interested in expanding that series. This seemed the perfect opportunity to create the book John and I had talked about and to reach the broadest range of readers. At last we were under way.

The first step was to decide what life's ten most important questions are. This was a matter calling for some serious brainstorming. Since the book was intended for a wide variety of people, we needed to choose practical issues that must be faced by each one of us. We weren't after the type of theoretical concerns that a postgraduate philosophy student might wonder about. Our focus was on the questions that would be most meaningful and important to the person who lived next door, or the one we might pass on the street.

Once we had identified suitable areas to look into, we had to go back to the Cayce readings to make sure they actually addressed these issues. After all, the readings had been given during the first half of the century. Are the questions that were asked of Edgar Cayce then ones that people are still concerned with today? And are the answers he gave fifty years ago applicable to life in the modern world?

About the questions, we need not have worried. Throughout time, people have faced certain fundamental issues related to the basic conditions of human life, and the people of Edgar Cayce's day sought advice and guidance on many matters that are still of vital importance. Included here are ultimate questions about the existence of God, the purpose of life, and what happens to us when it's over. Also included are personal, day-to-day questions, such as how to overcome our negative attitudes, maintain physical health, and find fulfillment in our work and our interpersonal relationships.

As to whether the answers Edgar Cayce gave to life's important questions are still valid and useful today, that is something that must be determined by each individual person. All I can do is invite the reader to take a look and find out for himself.

Who Was Edgar Cayce?

At this point, the reader unfamiliar with the story of Edgar Cayce is likely to be asking several natural questions. Who was Edgar Cayce? What exactly did he do? How did he do it? And where did the information that he gave come from? Let's take a bit of time now to get acquainted with the man and his work.

Edgar Cayce was born on a farm near Hopkinsville, Kentucky, on March 18, 1877, the first of five children born to Leslie B. Cayce and his wife, Carrie. The couple raised their family in the Christian Church, an offshoot of

Presbyterianism. Carrie Cayce, a gentle, patient woman, was very supportive of her son and exerted a strong influence throughout his early years.

Edgar Cayce spent his boyhood on the family farm, where the natural, open spaces agreed with him. At an early age, my grandfather developed a powerful interest in the Bible. As a child, he loved to hear and later to read the stories of the biblical heroes. When he was ten years old he received a Bible of his own, and shortly thereafter he resolved to read it through in its entirety once for every year he lived.

This love of the Bible was one aspect of a strong Christian faith that was an important focal point of Edgar Cayce's whole life. As an adult he regularly taught Sunday school, and the guidance and inspiration he found in the Scriptures were supplemented by a rich prayer life, through which he continually sought to discover and align himself with God's will.

His constant Bible reading aside, as a youth Edgar Cayce was no scholar. He had trouble keeping his mind on his lessons in school, and when called upon to read or recite he would often be lost in his own private thoughts.

In many ways, Edgar Cayce's childhood was a simple one, typical of most boys' of his time and place. But on occasion his unusual abilities showed themselves. At an early age, for instance, he reported seeing and conversing with his grandfather, whose accidental death Edgar had witnessed when he was four years old. Some time later, he discovered that by sleeping with his head on his school books he could learn their entire contents.

One day the young Edgar Cayce was alone in the woods, reading his Bible. There he experienced a vision of a beautiful lady who told him that his prayers had been answered. She asked him what he would like. Though a bit frightened, he managed to say that he wanted to be able to help other people, especially children who were ill. This desire to be of aid to others was a characteristic that would last throughout Edgar Cayce's life. All during the years in which he gave readings, his primary concern was that the information that came through him be valid and truly beneficial to the people for whom it was given.

The first time my grandfather's special gifts were used in healing occurred after he had been hit with a ball. The shock to his system caused him to act strangely for the rest of the day. After he had been put to bed, he explained to his parents in a serious voice what had happened and what could be done to eliminate the problem. His parents did as he directed. When Edgar awakened the next morning he was feeling fine, though he had no memory of anything that had happened since he'd been struck.

Edgar Cayce left school at the age of sixteen and began working on the family farm. He stayed there until he was twenty-two, when he moved into the town of Hopkinsville. There he got a job at a bookstore, where he met Gertrude Evans. The two young people fell in love and became engaged to be married.

But Edgar felt that before he could be married he should have some savings set aside. During his young adulthood he would take jobs selling shoes, as an insurance salesman, and in various bookstores and photographic studios. He discovered he had a knack for photography, and for a time he thought that this would be his life's work. From Hopkinsville he traveled to Saint Louis and later to Bowling Green, Kentucky, looking for a good-paying job that would provide the funds he thought he needed in order to settle down and marry Gertrude. But somehow financial stability always eluded him.

Shortly before his twenty-third birthday, Edgar Cayce lost his voice. For over a year he was unable to speak above a hoarse whisper. Various local doctors tried to treat his condition, to no avail. The breakthrough came when Al Layne, a local man who had taken correspondence courses in suggestive therapeutics and in osteopathy, guided him through a form of self-hypnosis.

Edgar went into a self-induced trance and described the cause of his problem in a normal tone of voice. He added that the condition could be removed through suggestion. Layne made the appropriate suggestion, and when my grandfather awakened, he was able to speak normally. Edgar Cayce had just given what many regard as his first health reading. He himself had no conscious recollection of what had occurred while he was in trance.

Al Layne suggested that if my grandfather could accurately describe conditions in his own body and how to treat them, perhaps he could perform the same service for others. They agreed to try a test reading for a health problem of Layne's, and the results were successful. The upshot of this experiment was that Al Layne and Edgar Cayce formed a partnership. My grandfather gave readings to diagnose the problems of patients and determine what treatments would be effective, and Layne took down the readings and supervised the treatments.

Edgar Cayce was at first very hesitant about this arrangement. He didn't understand his unusual ability and, since his formal schooling was limited and his conscious knowledge of medicine practically nonexistent, he couldn't imagine where his information came from. He was very worried that while in trance he might prescribe something that would be harmful to someone, and he decided that if anyone were ever hurt by following the advice of his readings, he would stop giving them.

In the end, three things convinced him to go along with Layne's plan. First, he didn't want to miss the opportunity to help others. Second, he had been assured that Layne knew enough medicine from his correspondence courses to recognize any potentially harmful measures the readings might suggest. And third, whenever he considered pulling out of the venture, he started to lose his voice again.

Since at this time Edgar Cayce steadfastly refused to accept payment for using his gift, he continued to support himself with his photography. Twice a day he would leave the photo studio to go to the offices Layne had rented for readings. It was soon discovered that the person for whom the reading was being given need not be physically present. Distance was no barrier to the functioning of Edgar Cayce's ability. No description of symptoms or case history was necessary. All that was needed for my grandfather to be able to deliver a reading was the subject's name and location.

Before beginning a reading, Edgar Cayce would loosen his collar, belt, and shoelaces and remove his cufflinks. He'd lie down on his back on the couch, with his hands folded over his abdomen. His respiration would deepen as he stilled his mind, and he would close his eyes and "sleep." The appropriate suggestion to begin the reading would be given. There would be a moment or two of silence, and then the information would start to come forth. Frequently, it would be salted with quotations and illustrations from the Bible that was such an important part of Edgar Cayce's waking life. The diction was often scriptural, and at times the phrasing was convoluted and difficult to interpret. At the conclusion of the reading the suggestion to awaken would be given, and my grandfather would come out of his trance.

Throughout this early period, Al Layne served as both the conductor and the stenographer for the readings, giving the appropriate suggestions, asking relevant questions, and taking down the information. Later, Edgar's father and then Gertrude Evans Cayce would be his most frequent conductors, and a professional stenographer would be hired.

During the time Edgar Cayce worked with Al Layne, he moved from Hopkinsville to Bowling Green, where he got a better-paying job at a bookstore. On June 17, 1903, at the age of twenty-six, he was at last in a position to marry Gertrude, and the couple set up their home in Bowling Green. In time they would have three sons: my father, Hugh Lynn Cayce; Milton Porter Cayce; and Edgar Evans Cayce.

At first, word of Edgar Cayce's unusual abilities spread slowly. Whatever notice he drew was mostly local. A down-to-earth and humble man, during the first part of his stay in Bowling Green he sought to keep his friends from discovering his remarkable gifts. He enjoyed being liked for himself, and, understandably, he didn't want anyone to consider him a freak.

Any plans my grandfather might have had for living in pleasant obscurity were severely disrupted on October 9, 1910. On that date, a two-page story appeared in the *New*

York Times, complete with headlines and photographs. The story grew out of a report authored by Dr. Wesley Ketchum, a young homeopath who had set up office in Hopkinsville and obtained a few readings from Edgar Cayce.

As a result of the *Times* article and stories in other newspapers, my grandfather's abilities received nationwide attention. At the urging of his father, Ketchum, and a hotel owner in Hopkinsville, my grandfather entered into a partnership with them as a psychic diagnostician. When he got to Hopkinsville, he found nearly ten thousand letters requesting readings, many of them with payment enclosed. The partnership was to last a little over a year.

This was a period of trial for my grandfather. In 1911, his second son, Milton Porter Cayce, died soon after birth. Shortly thereafter, Gertrude's health began to fail. The trouble was diagnosed as tuberculosis, and at one point doctors gave her just a week to live. Granddad gave a reading for her, and when the treatments it described were followed my grandmother recovered.

The dissolution of my grandfather's partnership with Dr. Ketchum and the others was not a happy one. One of the concerns that had greatly troubled the partners was the difficulty of finding doctors who would administer the treatments prescribed in the readings. Typically, as soon as a doctor found out the source of the information, he would refuse to follow its recommendations. What was needed was a fully equipped hospital, staffed by members of all branches of the healing profession, who were both thoroughly trained in their medical specialties and convinced of the readings' validity. In order to get funds for such a hospital, Dr. Ketchum began taking readings to obtain information that could be used to financial advantage. When Edgar Cayce discovered what was being done, he withdrew from the partnership.

This disagreement highlighted something that had been causing my grandfather misgivings for quite some time. While in trance, he had no conscious knowledge of the questions asked or what he answered. It was possible for the person conducting the reading to slip in questions, and sometimes entire readings, on subjects that Edgar Cayce felt constituted an improper use of his abilities. Sometimes months would go by before he found out what was being done. What he needed was someone to conduct the readings whom he could trust implicitly. Finally, it occurred to him that the perfect person for the job was the one he was married to. My grandmother regularly conducted Granddad's readings for the last thirty years of his life.

During the second decade of the century, Edgar Cayce's readings grew in both fame and range of topics considered. Requests came in by mail from all over the country, and from a number of foreign nations as well. It was discovered that Granddad could give advice not only about a person's physical condition, but about his mental outlook and vocational choices as well. During this period, mental/spiritual readings were added to the physical discourses, which continued to be the mainstay of the practice, and readings on world affairs soon followed.

Two important developments occurred in 1923, each of which had a lasting impact on Edgar Cayce's work. That year my grandfather decided to hire a regular stenographer to take the readings down. He chose a young

woman named Gladys Davis for the job. Gladys devoted
the rest of her life to the work, staying with the family
during some very trying times, recording most of the
readings Edgar Cayce gave during the remainder of his
days, and making a valuable contribution to their preser-
vation after he had died.

The second major event resulted from the involvement
of Arthur Lammers, of Dayton, Ohio. Lammers had a
deep interest in subjects like philosophy, comparative
religion, and metaphysics, and he felt that the answers to
his esoteric questions could be obtained through Edgar
Cayce. He received several readings in which he explored these areas. Of the many concepts that came out
of these discourses, the one that had the most powerful
effect was reincarnation.

When first confronted with the readings' mention of
this subject, Edgar Cayce was skeptical. It seemed to go
against the tenets of the Bible-centered Christianity that
was at the core of his life. But in time he came to accept
this belief. A whole new class of readings emerged,
describing the subject's former appearances on earth and
the ways in which those earlier experiences were influ-
encing the present lifetime. This type of discourse came
to be known as the life reading.

At the request of Lammers, Edgar Cayce moved to
Dayton with his family and Gladys Davis. Unfortunately,
Lammers was soon beset by financial difficulties. This
produced a very lean period for the Cayce family. They
managed to survive the hard times, largely by means of
income generated by the medical and life readings.

Among the people helped by these readings was Morton
Blumenthal, a successful New York stockbroker. Like

Lammers, Blumenthal was interested in metaphysical matters. He received a long series of life readings and philosophical discourses. In 1925, Blumenthal financed the family's move to Virginia Beach, Virginia. For several years the readings had been saying that was where Edgar Cayce's work should be conducted.

In 1927, the Association of National Investigators was incorporated to investigate psychic abilities, particularly those of Edgar Cayce; to determine how such abilities could be practically applied; and to educate each individual in the active use of the mind's higher powers. One of the main agencies through which this purpose was to be achieved was a hospital in which the physical treatments described in the Cayce medical readings would be administered. Construction of the hospital was financed largely by Morton Blumenthal. The hospital was dedicated on November 11, 1928, and admitted its first patient the next day.

A second phase of the association's work was intended to be accomplished by an institution of higher learning, Atlantic University. Perhaps it was a case of trying to do too much too soon. At any rate, the cost of maintaining the two facilities, plus the financial difficulty brought on by the Depression, put a serious strain on Blumenthal's resources. His support was withdrawn, and the Association of National Investigators ceased all its operations. The hospital was closed on February 28, 1931. For Edgar Cayce this was a heavy blow; the hospital had been a longtime dream, and during its brief period of operation it had proved its value.

Once again my grandfather and his family faced a period of hardship. But Edgar Cayce determined to continue offering his special kind of help to others. He contacted everyone on his personal mailing list, asking if they thought his work was worth establishing a new organization to take the place of the association that had folded. The response was enthusiastic. In July of 1931 the Association for Research and Enlightenment was founded.

With the support of A.R.E. members, the work of Edgar Cayce entered a period of slow growth. Under the energetic managing of my father, Hugh Lynn Cayce, the A.R.E. increased its efforts to investigate the special abilities of Edgar Cayce and make their benefits available to others. Requests for readings continued to come in— not always in staggering numbers, but steadily.

During much of the 1930s, Edgar Cayce lived rather quietly at his home in Virginia Beach. He received a few visitors, both friends and newcomers interested in the work he was doing. His routine included two reading sessions a day, morning and afternoon, and he devoted several hours daily to reading and answering the mail. Among his hobbies were fishing, gardening, canning fruits and vegetables, and doing carpentry. Evenings, he relaxed at home with his wife, playing cards and listening to the radio. As always, his Bible was a steady companion.

With the onset of World War II and the 1943 publication of the Edgar Cayce biography *There Is a River*, the pace picked up considerably; at times, the number of applications for readings reached fifteen hundred per day. Everyone felt pressed to keep up with this growing mountain of work. Often Granddad was busy until ten in the evening or later.

The readings themselves warned that if he didn't cut

back on the number of readings he was giving—and, more important, on the amount of worrying he was doing over the growing backlog—his health would suffer. But my grandfather was unable to ignore the huge number of pleas for help that reached him.

In August of 1944 he collapsed from overwork. As directed by a reading he gave for himself, he and my grandmother went to a rest facility in Roanoke, Virginia. There he appeared to improve for a while. The last reading Edgar Cayce was ever to give, performed at Roanoke on September 17, 1944, held out hope for his recovery and eventual return to work; but it also stressed that continued rest from anxiety was crucial. A week later my grandfather suffered a stroke. In November he was returned to his home in Virginia Beach, where he died on January 3, 1945, of pulmonary edema. Three months later Gertrude Cayce died, on Easter Sunday morning.

Understanding the Readings

It's difficult to judge the total number of discourses Edgar Cayce transmitted between March 1901 and September 1944, but more than fourteen thousand of them were stenographically recorded and have been preserved by the A.R.E. These collected readings alone were given for over six thousand seekers. In order to protect the identities of the people for whom they were given, each of the collected readings has been numbered according to the individual or group who received it and the sequence in which it was received. Reading 900-15, for example, is the fifteenth reading given for the person designated by the number 900.

A quick survey of the readings reveals that they cover a very broad range of topics. Physical readings, given to evaluate the subject's health and to diagnose and guide the treatment of bodily ailments, constitute the largest class of discourses. Another extensive grouping is the life readings, which trace the subject's previous incarnations and indicate how the present lifetime is being influenced by earlier experiences. Large numbers of readings were given to provide business advice, mental and spiritual guidance, and interpretations of dreams. And certain series of readings were given to groups of people seeking to achieve specific purposes. One series, for instance, was given to direct the work of preserving, investigating, and disseminating the material that came through Edgar Cayce; another was obtained by a group endeavoring to draw closer to God and to develop their own psychic abilities.

There were apparently two basic sources Edgar Cayce tapped into in order to receive this wealth of information. The first to be described in the readings is the subconscious mind. According to the Cayce material, the subconscious minds of all individuals are interconnected. What is known to one subconscious is accessible to all. Edgar Cayce had the ability to overcome the limitations of the personal self and attune to and receive information from the subconscious minds of others. In addition, he had the uncommon ability to transmit this material from the subconscious in a way that was intelligible to the objective minds of those around him.

The second source of information available to Edgar

Cayce was described in later readings as the superconscious mind. This can be thought of as the level of mind at which each individual soul is aware of its relationship to God, in Whom there is all knowledge and wisdom. Attunement to the superconscious makes it possible to draw upon this source of infinite knowledge. Like communicating with other subconscious minds, this type of attunement entails moving beyond the bounds of the self; the difference is that at the superconscious level contact is made with universal awareness, rather than with other individual intelligences.

Because the superconscious mind communicates with the infinite, omniscient Creator, information received from this level is unlimited and infallible. Edgar Cayce's own waking attitude reflected this. At various times in his life he expressed doubts about his own abilities and the origin of the information he gave. But once he became convinced that material was proceeding from universal awareness, he had complete confidence in it.

At the superconscious level, we can gain access to the Akashic Record, a universal chronicle of everything that has ever been thought, said, and done by everybody who has ever lived. The Akashic Record—which is also referred to in the readings as the Book of Life or the Book of God's Remembrance—can be thought of as a manifestation of the Creator's eternal omniscience. It can be read by anyone making proper attunement to the superconscious mind.

This last point is an extremely striking and hopeful one. Far from extolling Edgar Cayce as a uniquely talented individual, the readings affirm that we all have the potential to accomplish what he did. Subconscious

contact is available to all minds, and the omniscience of
the superconscious exists for each one of us. What is
needed in order to communicate with these levels is the
ability to lay aside our identification with the limited,
personal self, and to attune ourselves to God, the universal source. It is true that this ability was much more
developed in Edgar Cayce than it is in most of us. But
ultimately, the sources he drew upon and the kind of
information he received are within the reach of everybody.

The guidance given in the Cayce material is nothing if
not practical. Over and over again it stresses that knowledge in itself is of little value; it is the practical application of knowledge that matters. Our spiritual progress
doesn't depend on our understanding and accepting the
readings' view of creation, reincarnation, or anything
else. What counts is how we live our daily lives—how
constructively we use the resources the Creator has given
us, and how lovingly we treat the people around us. The
two keys to successful living are attunement to the will of
God and service to our fellow man.

In answer to universal questions about the existence of
God and the purpose of life, the Edgar Cayce material
conveys the hope that comes from knowing that our path
has direction and that it leads to a destination worth
reaching. In answering such personal questions as how to
overcome guilt and to work at our highest capacity, the
readings offer concrete suggestions that can help us see
the next step more clearly.

Cayce's hope and that help can do a lot to smooth the
journey, both for the newcomer encountering the Cayce
material for the first time, and for the old-timer seeking

fresh perspectives on familiar ideas. If *Edgar Cayce Answers Life's 10 Most Important Questions* can impart this encouragement and aid to the reader, it will have fulfilled its purpose.

—*Charles Thomas Cayce*
January 1989
Virginia Beach,
Virginia

INTRODUCTION

As an investigative journalist for national periodicals and book publishers I have explored many strange and unusual stories. Often I first encounter them in small news items buried deep inside the newspaper, where they are likely to be glossed over by the casual reader. However, I have found that by doing some heavy legwork, a fascinating true story often emerges.

For instance, I once ran across a small-type headline for a one-inch item in the *New York Times* that read: "ENTIRE FRENCH VILLAGE GOES INSANE." This turned out to be an absorbing, factual medical detective story.

Later, I found a small *Times* item headlined, "STATE HIGHWAY PATROLMEN IN NEW MEXICO, TEXAS, AND NEW HAMPSHIRE REPORT SCORES OF UFO SIGHTINGS." The book that came from it brought new respect to the UFO subject.

A third intriguing headline, "NEW DEADLY AFRICAN VIRUS KILLS YALE SCIENTISTS ON CONTACT, turned out to be a real-life *Andromeda Strain*, while a fourth head-

23

line, "EASTERN AIRLINES PILOTS REPORT GHOST PILOT ON JUMBO JETS," led me into an investigation that opened my eyes in unexpected ways. This was my first intimation that there could indeed be some form of existence after death.

After I had put in a year's worth of research and travel on each of these four tiny news items, I was able to write four successful full-sized nonfiction books, including Book of the Month and Literary Guild selections. But in the process, I was plunged into regions, like the psychic, that are often thought to be taboo for a journalist. Nonetheless, I have found that careful research with an open mind can unfold gripping stories of genuine value to the reader.

One reason for the taboo, I suspect, is that the journalist on the daily beat does not have enough time to dig thoroughly into such subject matter. If the day-by-day newsbeat journalist *did* have the time, he or she might end up being as surprised and delighted as I have been.

In approaching a story that lies on the frontiers of science, it is important to maintain the attitude of a benevolent skeptic. It is also important to keep in mind that there are two enemies of any story that delves into the unknown regions beyond conventional knowledge.

The first enemy is the *destructive* skeptic, who refuses, simply out of prejudice, to even consider reasonable and rational evidence. I encountered one such skeptic, who immediately began explaining away all the UFO sightings I had confirmed in my interviews with seasoned Air Force pilots in Exeter, New Hampshire. But he hadn't even taken the trouble to go there. His explanation was that the sightings "simply couldn't be."

The other basic enemy of stories that dip into the

unknown is the gullible, enthusiastic believer who embraces every spook-and-kook story with open arms, failing to check out facts with full caution. The overenthusiasm of this kind of believer is as damaging to the credibility of these interesting stories as is the negativity of the destructive skeptic.

That's why I try to be a benevolent skeptic: my skepticism sees to it that I investigate stories thoroughly, while the benevolence I try to maintain helps me stay open to the widest range of possibilities.

I first stumbled onto the story of Edgar Cayce several years ago, quite by accident. A friend of mine had urged me to read two books about Edgar Cayce: *The Sleeping Prophet,* by Jess Stearn, and *There Is a River,* by Thomas Sugrue. Both writers were solid journalists who had the talent to make the incredible story of Edgar Cayce seem credible. Several million people who have read these books apparently felt the same way.

My first encounter with the books left me stunned. Edgar Cayce had supposedly produced incredible works of psychic healing. He had counseled thousands of perplexed and anguished people who desperately sought his advice. Here, I read, was a man who could ''see'' (with his mind's eye) ailing subjects thousands of miles away, who could startle seasoned medical experts with his accomplishments. All this was too much to be believed.

The reported accomplishments of the late Edgar Cayce struck me as impossible, even outrageously impossible. As the old-time radio comedian Colonel Stoopnagle would have put it, I wanted to look for an eleven-foot pole because this was a story I wouldn't touch with a ten-foot pole. But I soon found that the cautiously evaluated medical evidence of Cayce's accomplishments was strong, almost airtight. So here I was, once again faced with a story that seemed impossible to believe, yet once I started to dig into the documented facts, it was impossible *not* to believe it. I was intrigued, to say the least, but the Edgar Cayce story had already been told well by his biographers. As a writer, I felt there was nothing of great value I could add.

And yet, years later, when I visited with Charles Thomas Cayce as part of my research for another story, I felt a strong pull to tackle a story about Edgar Cayce, perhaps emphasizing some special facet of his remarkable work. Dr. Cayce was encouraging. The problem for me was finding some new area that reflected a critical need on the part of those who looked to Cayce's works for help and guidance. I didn't want to cover old ground.

When an opportunity arose to proceed with the project, Charles Thomas was good enough to arrange a staff meeting to help me probe for the best ideas for writing this book. The question at hand was, What were the most frequently asked of the questions that came to Edgar Cayce in his daily mail? The collective experience of the A.R.E. staff was invaluable to me as we sifted through the Cayce readings and correspondence in a search for the questions that would benefit the widest spectrum of readers.

I soon learned that the Cayce medical miracles were only part of the picture. His insights into the blistering, agonizing questions that arise in the course of everyday living have proved to be equally helpful in alleviating mental, emotional, and spiritual anguish, not just poor physical health.

In the modern, efficient library of the A.R.E. headquarters I found copies of over fourteen thousand of Cayce's psychic readings, dictated for some six thousand troubled seekers who wrote Cayce for advice over a span of some fifty years. Being no expert on the material—I look at myself as more of a companion with you, the reader, than as a guide on this exploration of the Cayce wisdom—I relied heavily on the expertise of the A.R.E. staff to show the way.

It took a lengthy assault on the archives to ferret out what seemed to be the ten most important questions on the minds of a wide demographic and geographic sample of people. The selection process was interesting, however, because it provided a substantial base for this book. What's important to a secretary in Kansas, I figured, might not be important to a homemaker from Scarsdale, New York. Surprisingly, what I discovered was that, regardless of occupation, locale, or background, certain basic questions remained important to a broad majority of Cayce's correspondents.

As the A.R.E. staff helped me in the huge task of screening the files for the answers Cayce gave to these ten questions, there was no sign whatsoever of a "cult" mentality; no pressure brought to bear in an effort to influence my own beliefs. I have always felt that any belief structure that becomes overinstitutionalized, or that spawns a sense of passionate advocacy, does so at its own peril. At the A.R.E., I was relieved to see, the atmosphere is that of a relaxed and open college campus where knowledge is sought, prejudice and intolerance are avoided, and exploration of all points of view is conducted with an open-minded attitude. The staff, along with Charles Thomas Cayce, seemed content to let the extraordinary deeds of Edgar Cayce speak for themselves.

To me, what sets Cayce apart from the conventional therapist, psychiatrist, or pastor is the palpable evidence that he was able to reach into a level of consciousness above and beyond the confined and confining finite mind. To try to understand how and why the "sleeping" Edgar Cayce could answer critically important questions for all of us, I had to explore the fundamentals of his beliefs.

Cayce's basic platform was simple: All is One. But the carpentry that holds this platform together is enormously complex, as we'll see as we explore his answers to life's ten most important questions. For now, let me just say that I was able to accept his platform because it doesn't require a major leap of faith; it doesn't demand that I subscribe to any slogan, swear any half-understood fidelity, grovel on my knees in front of some Authority Figure. Nor am I required to memorize any prayer that someone else tells me is obligatory. All it says is, "Here's an idea to ponder. Accept it if you feel inclined to do so."

I hope I've made it clear that I've approached the story of Edgar Cayce with respect but with caution. If I succeed in showing how the mind of a benevolent skeptic (like mine) can receive fresh and abundant new insights simply by examining the Edgar Cayce evidence, this book will serve its purpose.

I have found that Cayce makes it possible to find mental and spiritual stability in a calm and unemotional way. This is what appeals to me most; I never could relate to the frenetic evangelism that often infects the spiritual quest.

If you are just beginning to become acquainted with Edgar Cayce's works, and are an outsider as I am, I hope you will enjoy exploring Cayce's expansive outlook that has cast such a brilliant light on the self, the universe, and the mysteries of both.

QUESTION 1

Is There a God?

I've always been envious of "true believers," people with pure, unquestioning, abiding faith. I've run into many of them in my time, and while I've envied them, they've also left me skeptical and puzzled. This was certainly true of some missionaries I once met deep in the heart of equatorial Africa.

A mysterious new viral disease had appeared in the remote village of Lassa, Nigeria. A blood specimen taken from a missionary who had died of the disease was sent to medical researchers at Yale University. Within ten days of examining the specimen several of the researchers were dead. The blood was considered so dangerous that it had to be incinerated. Further, reports from Nigeria said that medical missionaries were dying within ten days of having even the slightest contact with the victims.

Fascinated, I set out to do a story on this new disease, riding fifteen hundred miles in a Land Rover to reach Lassa, though as a devout hypochondriac I was scared to death. I couldn't understand how the missionaries were able to continue with their work when their associates were dropping like flies around them. The answer they gave me was simple: "We believe in God, we believe we are called to help others, and we will continue to do so. We put all our faith in God."

How were they able to do this? I didn't know. I couldn't wait to get out of the place—which is what I did as quickly as I could.

But their determined faith remained in my mind. It puzzled me and made me envious, because I saw no way I could achieve such an outlook. You can't just order yourself to have faith; you have to feel it viscerally.

It's no wonder, then, that among the many questions Edgar Cayce fielded in his flood of daily mail, a persistent one, whether asked explicitly or simply implied, was the blunt and direct, "Is there a God?"

The question is not as abstract as it sounds. For many of the letter writers it had a direct bearing on their everyday lives. And as we'll discover, Cayce's answers to this first question provide a wellspring of answers to all the other questions that follow in this book. God—and the nature of God—permeates every facet of personal living in the most tangible way. To Cayce, the First Cause of the Universe—God—is not only omniscient and omnipresent but provides an infinite reservoir of divine energy that we can draw on to solve problems of every kind.

This should not be a roadblock to those of you who are not religious. Cayce's concept of God is so broad that it embraces both the sacred and the secular; it can have an impact on the believer, the puzzled, the doubter, and the unbeliever alike. The Cayce material was the first thing ever to help me make a quantum leap in my search for a rational understanding of how and why existence came about, and of the Great Creator that set everything in motion. Cayce has been instrumental in persuading my reluctant mind that spiritual reality exists and that it might actually be the dominant reality, over and above the material world perceived by our five limited senses.

For anyone who enjoyed raising hell in Sunday school as much as I did, this is quite a leap.

Clearing Away Obstacles

Because I feel more like a companion with you, the reader, rather than a guide on this exploratory trek into the mystic mind of Edgar Cayce, it might help for me to cite some of the difficulties I've encountered in accepting spiritual ideas—in this case, my difficulties in accepting the simple existence of God—and, of course, to share those things that have helped me move toward acceptance.

My earliest attempts at seeking the spiritual were effectively blunted by an overexuberant, pulpit-pounding Presbyterian minister. In my later years, my fondness for a gourmet dinner, a zinging extra-dry martini, and an occasional indulgence of the flesh set up a strong armor plate against any weak flashes of spiritual light and insight I might have had. For someone with a somewhat "pagan" turn of mind like mine, it's much easier to have faith in measurable scientific concepts than it is to make a leap of faith into belief in concepts of the divine.

Cayce helps us make this leap by letting us look for God through several windows.

But even before helping to explain what God *is*, Cayce helped me along my path by relieving me of false notions about what God is supposed to be—but isn't.

In trying to answer the question "Is there a God?" we first must picture what image of God would supply a satisfactory answer. We need an image of God that makes sense to us. Over and over in my exploration of Cayce's concepts I found myself relying on visual images to help me understand and accept cosmic ideas; sometimes, it seems, the cosmic is more effectively communicated through metaphor than through cold, logical language. In the same way, there are some images, I found, that can stand in the way of understanding.

Despite Michelangelo's incredible genius as a painter, I've had to spend a long time and a lot of energy shaking off the burden of his anthropomorphic image of God—an imposing old man, complete with flowing white beard, floating nebulously in a very real sky. I'm sure God must have patted the great painter on the shoulder for his noble effort, but I'm not sure He was altogether pleased with being squeezed into such a fleshly figure. Unfortunately, Michelangelo's logic didn't measure up to his stunning ability with the paintbrush. If God is omniscient and omnipresent and beyond the puny boundaries of space and time, He is unlikely to be confined to a human figure—even one as imposing as the figure on the ceiling of the Sistine Chapel. As we'll see later, Cayce does indeed speak of man as being in the image of God, but in an abstract sense that's less confining than a mere human body.

A God I Can Live With

Who then—or what—is God?

The First Cause, the Universal Forces, the Creative Force—these are some of the terms Edgar Cayce used to communicate the essence of God; each is another approach to expressing his basic understanding that *All is One*.

Cayce's view of God as the First Cause is something I find persuasive because it is consistent with the big bang theory advanced by scientists to explain the origin of the cosmos: a huge burst of energy that started the whole works in motion. On a metaphysical level I can accept it because *something* had to be the First Cause or we wouldn't be here; the solar system wouldn't be here and life wouldn't be here; and neither you nor I would be here.

Cayce also calls this the Original Creative Energy: an infinite pool of energy that exists everywhere—whether we want it to be here or not. Reasoning from this premise, we see that if this great energy is everywhere, if it's all-inclusive, you and I have got to be part of it whether we want to be or not, and it doesn't really matter what we call it: it is *all there is*. Viewed this way, these forces are extensions or manifestations of the one God, evidence of Cayce's conviction that all is one in God. Or, as the biblical doctrine puts it, that in God we live and move and have our being, and that God is one "through whom and for whom everything exists."

Now let's take this reasoning one step further. If everything that exists comes from and is part of this Original Creative Energy, then life and consciousness, including self-awareness, emerged from it too. And from this conception flows Cayce's simple definition of life itself: Life is the consciousness of existence.

Our Relation to the First Cause

As we'll see from the answers that Cayce's readings offer to life's great questions, the source of many of our problems as human beings is that we have allowed ourselves to separate from the First Cause. We've become detached from it, and our basic job is to rejoin it completely, the way we were before we came into consciousness. Our job is to steer ourselves back to that state and merge with it. We retain our self-awareness but align our purpose to the greater design of the universe.

"But is that possible?" my skeptic's mind asks as it considers the denseness of our physical bodies. Here one of my mental images steps in to help me picture the possible. The body—or any chunk of physical matter—is not as dense as we think. The atoms we consist of are mainly empty space. There's no argument about that. In fact, the fundamental building block of matter isn't matter at all. It's the photon, and the photon is simply light, or energy.

Einstein was the first to point out that matter isn't matter at all; it's more or less frozen light in the form of "force fields." Viewed that way, it's possible to picture the universe and all its infinite photons as pure energy and hence as permeable as a beam of sunlight. Our dense bodies too, therefore, can be imagined as only a cloud of photons, a cloud of light that can move out to rejoin the

First Cause as smoothly as two puffy clouds merging to become one.

Think how relaxing that would be: to rest in the womb of our origin, to effortlessly blend with it and harmonize with the design and direction of the Universal Forces rather than, as Shakespeare put it, "troubling deaf heaven with bootless cries."

"But purpose?" the skeptic in me asks. "Is there really purpose to these Creative Forces? A grand design and immutable laws of harmony?" It's not too difficult, I find, to look at this pragmatically. No such machinery as the untold number of galaxies, stars, and planets could possibly survive without these immutable laws. Nor could the billions of cells in our physical bodies. There would be only chaos. As a result I don't find it hard to accept Cayce's premise that all is harmonized by God's will and intelligence, and that we can find peace and reassurance by blending with it instead of fighting it.

We can do this, Cayce teaches, because all knowledge, all information in the universe, is *there*. It exists. It is complete like the laws of mathematics, which are simply sitting there for us to fathom. We need only attune ourselves to it by placing the self totally in harmony with it.

Is this really possible to do? Throughout my career as an explorer of paranormal material, I've always felt the need to turn to leading objective thinkers—scientists and traditional philosophers—to find support for transcendental notions. I've followed this course in my exploration of the Cayce material as well, and so throughout this book I have included the thoughts of scientists and philosophers who have helped me on my journey toward acceptance.

One such scientist is David Bohm, a physicist whose work at the University of London earned him worldwide acclaim as a Nobel laureate. In his illuminating book *Wholeness and the Implicate Order,* in which he implies that science and mysticism might possibly be joined together, he postulates "an explicate order of the universe where everything is interconnected with everything else." He helps us visualize this concept by comparing it to a hologram: a photographic picture in which every point on the slide contains all the information about the entire picture. Chop up the slide into tiny pieces, then shine a holographic laser beam through one single piece, and the whole picture will appear. Similarly, any basic particle of matter can know instantly what happens to its "mate" elsewhere in the universe, regardless of distance. For me, what emerges from Bohm's reasoning is scientific support for Cayce's view of the oneness of everything, that "All is One," and for the notion that we can actually tune in to that All.

According to Cayce, since the conscious mind is imprisoned in the physical body, only the unconscious mind can transcend that barrier. To do this, we must have a selfless, constructive intention to move beyond the bounds of ordinary finite existence. We must have a total desire to blend with the oneness of the universe, to blend with the All-ness of it. This All-ness is Cayce's concept of God.

This is our task, then, and the answer to our problems: to understand that we are actually a part of God and that we can rejoin Him; to surrender ourselves to this great source-force and put our human will to work harmonizing with it. We must tune in to the realm of the infinite divinity, which is the realm of pure spirit where the "real" reality resides.

God the Creator and Parent

None of this should suggest, however, that Cayce regarded God as an impersonal force. On the contrary, when God launched existence, launching us with it as a part of His intelligence, He created each of us as an individual soul that composes the real spiritual individual, above and beyond the physical body but still part of it during our earthly sojourn. We always remain part of God's purpose, and as such we are co-workers with God, following his grand design for the universe. But as our Maker and Creator, God is literally our parent and naturally has the love of a parent for its offspring. God's love for creation has palpable reality. Further, universal love remains the essence of all consciousness. We in turn have the filial duty to return this love in the form of love for each other as well as for God who created us. The base of Cayce's conviction then is twofold: God is One, but God is also Love.

Now let's listen in and hear how Cayce's own words communicate these ideas. One of his inquirers wrote to ask: "Is it correct when praying to think of God as impersonal force or energy, everywhere present; or as an intelligent listening mind which is aware of every individual on earth and who intimately knows everyone's needs and how to meet them?"

In his usual biblical intonations Cayce replied: "Both! For He is also the energies in the finite moving in material manifestation. He is also the Infinite with the awareness. And thus as ye attune thy own consciousness, thy own awareness, the unfoldment of the presence within beareth witness with the presence without. And as the Son gave, 'I and the Father are one,' then ye come to know that ye and thy Father are one, as ye abide in Him.'' Cayce refers here to Jesus' desire that we, like He, become attuned to the Creative Forces within us.

That God cares about us, the souls that he has created and that are a part of Him, Cayce made clear as he continued: ''Yet as we look into the infinity of space and time we realize there is then that force, that influence, also that is aware of the needs, and there is also that will, that choice given to the souls of men that they may be used, that they may be one, that they may apply same in their own feeble, weak ways perhaps; yet that comes to mean, comes to signify, comes to manifest in the lives of those that have lost their way, that very influence ye seek in the knowledge of God.''

But Cayce is speaking about more than the care God has for us, His children; he is speaking of the love and concern that we, as a part of God, should show for our fellow souls, a point Cayce drives home as the reading goes on: ''For until ye become as a savior, as a help to some soul that has lost hope, lost its way, ye do not fully comprehend the God within, the God without.''

This idea, that through our love of our fellow man we come to know the God that is within us all, is even more directly addressed in reading 262-130. The occasion, back in July of 1942, was a gathering of the first of the groups formed to study Edgar Cayce's teachings. Present in the Virginia Beach office were five members of the group, including Cayce's wife, Gertrude, his son Hugh Lynn Cayce, and his secretary, Gladys Davis, who recorded the session.

Once Cayce had entered his altered state of consciousness and was ready to reply from the depth of his unconscious mind, Mrs. Cayce began with the usual set of instructions:

"You will have before you members of group #1, present here, and their work on the lesson GOD-LOVE-MAN. You will give a further discourse on this lesson and suggestions in completing it."

Also as usual, Cayce began with his brief preamble: "Yes, we have the group as gathered here; as a group, as individuals, and their work on the lesson. . . .

"Is it true," he went on, "that God is love? Is it true that He is to each as a father? Is it true that He is to each as law? Is it true that we each know that influence, that law, that love, as a personal thing in our experience; and thus a personal God—not a personality but as a God that is known of self, that may be demonstrated in the life of the individual? . . .

"Love is qualified as an attribute of that force, power or influence known as God.

"Thus as man makes application of love in his daily experience, he finds God a personal God."

Cayce went on to add: "Let the next lesson be MAN'S RELATIONSHIP TO MAN, and the affirmation:

"FATHER GOD! LET ME, AS THY CHILD, SEE IN MY FELLOW MAN THE DIVINITY I WOULD WORSHIP IN THEE."

This is Cayce's constant theme: We are to look for the

divinity in others, "keeping self from condemning self or others."

Moving Toward Acceptance

Back in the days of Emerson and Thoreau and the remarkable cluster of transcendentalists in Concord, Massachusetts, Margaret Fuller (no relation to this writer) struggled with her own uneasiness about the nature of existence. She once remarked at dinner to her colleagues that she had finally found peace by realizing that, "I accept the universe." (Thomas Carlyle was said to have commented caustically, "She damn well better.")

Fuller's struggle reminds us that it is no easy job to accept the universe for what it is. It's true that Cayce's conception of the nature of God makes the task easier in the long run. And I guess from the ecclesiastical point of view you're not supposed to find God through reasoning but should go on faith alone. But that's not my way. So once again I've turned to scientists and philosophers to help me out.

I found some illuminating arguments in *How to Think About God: A Guide for the Pagan* by Mortimer Adler.

I should point out that Adler, the chairman of the *Encyclopedia Britannica*'s board of editors and the director of Chicago's Institute for Philosophical Research, has no direct connection with Edgar Cayce. I have taken the liberty of positioning them side by side because I found the parallels between their thoughts very heartening, showing how a mystical mind like Cayce's can interlock with an analytical one like Adler's to increase our understanding of existence.

Through the insights of his cosmic mind, Cayce is able to accept God at face value. Adler's approach is cool and logical. In his book he attacks the question with a powerful series of philosophical arguments—ones that can be pretty sticky going at times for the lay reader, but ones that in the end support Cayce's concepts.

Adler's conclusion is that a creative cause is necessary in order to explain the actualization of a "merely possible" cosmos—a cosmos that includes all of us. Since its creation could not be within the power of natural causes, we have to conclude that a supernatural cause, or God, exists. Further, God would have to be not only the creator but the *preserver* of the cosmos in order that it be sustained.

Even with this coolly logical approach, Adler, who like Cayce rejects the idea of an anthropomorphic God, does not shy away from speaking of God's love. He points out that to make something and preserve it is unquestionably an act of love, an argument reminiscent of Cayce's view of God as our actual parent. Adler tells us that to exist is good because "the superabundant goodness which is one with the infinite existence of the supreme being overflows into the limited goodness and finite existence of things that God brings into existence and preserves in existence."

Adler acknowledges that there are limits to how far logic can carry you; a philosophical gap remains that requires a leap of faith. In spite of this, Adler feels the effort to think logically about God is a worthwhile one since the God revealed by logic provides "reasonable grounds for belief."

From Acceptance to Surrender

Although Cayce has defined life as "the consciousness of existence," he has a companion definition in his reading numbered 5753-1, in which he says, "What is life? It is a manifestation of the First Cause—God." To accept God as the First Cause, then, is in effect to accept the universe. Cayce advises that we should release ourselves to both, just as Margaret Fuller struggled to do. Cayce, as we'll discover, offers many different ways to achieve this seemingly simple state. I've also developed a few of my own.

Surrendering myself to anything requires a talent I've never been able to master; every time I try I find it hard to let go of my ego. That's why I've never been a very good passenger. Purely because of my stubbornness, I like to be in control. So when Cayce suggests that we put ourselves completely in the hands of the Universal Forces—God—I find I have to conjure up imaginary situations to convince myself this is not such a bad idea. Some of them spring from my earliest memories.

As a youngster, I often crossed the Delaware River on a ferryboat out of Philadelphia. I remember complaining frequently to my mother that the boat was being steered off course; we weren't heading straight for the terminal on the opposite bank. Eventually we would dock at the right place, of course. What I didn't realize was that the captain, up on the bridge and out of my sight, knew about the unseen currents and tides and was making allowances for them. The boat was only *apparently* off course.

I have to remind myself of this when the planet earth seems headed in the wrong direction. And it seems to be that way much of the time. Since the earth's orbit is not running wild, somebody must be steering it who knows more than I do. Remembering what I've read of Cayce and Adler and the biblical wisdom of the past, it's possible for me to think that God is the captain and at the helm. So why not slide over and let God do the driving? A simple image like this helps me to understand what Cayce means when he tells us to surrender ourselves completely to God's will and the Universal Forces, to join in as a co-worker and companion.

Here's another useful image: I once was permitted to sit on the flight deck of a jumbo jet as it flew over the blackness of the Atlantic at night. The instrument panel glowed with a myriad of soft lights. The panel's indicators were utterly meaningless to my mind, but of course they were *everything* to the pilot. When I looked out past the lights, the magnificent array of stars seemed like a giant instrument panel in the sky. How foolish it would have been for me to grab the wheel from the pilot. How equally foolish to think I could take over the wheel of *Spaceship Earth*. Again, I might as well slide over and let God do the driving. And while I'm at it, I'll be free of so many navigational headaches if I align my will completely with God's.

I've got Edgar Cayce to thank for these simple images that have helped me believe in the existence of God after years of struggle. Many of my friends, so earthy, hearty, and physical that they too have trouble believing in God, say they've gained some insight because I've shared some of these images with them. That's why I don't feel off the track in sharing them with you; perhaps a look at my clumsy search for the reality of God will be of some help.

I remember one glorious fall day when, after studying some of Cayce's readings, I looked out over a hardwood forest blazing with autumnal foliage. The leaves were so rich with color that they hurt my eyes. They seemed to glow with the creative energy of the Universal Forces. Some, I saw, were being whipped off the branches by the wind, their job and lives completed as they fell to earth. What struck me was that each leaf was part of its tree; that through photosynthesis each had served the purpose of its tree before falling back to the earth from which the tree had sprung.

Here came an understanding of several of Cayce's ideas about our relationship with God: how, just like a leaf and its tree, we as created souls are part of God but separate too. How, just as the tree that created the leaves depended on the leaves as co-workers and companions, God created us as individuals who serve Him as companions and co-workers. How, just as the tree created seeds that carry the whole tree within them, we carry the spirit of God inside each of us since we are totally immersed in His divine energy.

Later that fall I looked at those same trees, bare now, with leafless limbs reaching upward as if in supplication to the skies, waiting to be reborn the following spring. Each tree showed in silence how it accepted the universe and the Creative Forces, which it allowed to permeate its existence. To me, these trees are a good example of why it makes sense to join fully the Universal Forces and surrender to them as Cayce urges.

I must admit that I still have a problem in reaching total surrender, but I am thankful to Cayce for leading me in the direction of such a peaceful and benign acceptance.

Another Guide: Jesus and The Christ Consciousness

Because Edgar Cayce was a Sunday school teacher most of his life, it is natural that he was steeped not only in a belief in God but in the Bible. This was reflected in the words he spoke and even in the tone of his voice while in an altered state of consciousness; his psychic readings ring with the echoes of biblical expression. He refers over and over to passages from the Bible, blending them with his own metaphysics.

One phrase that appears time and again in the readings, *Christ consciousness,* lies at the core of Cayce's guidance that we must focus our attention on the principles of Christ, which point the way to our full acceptance of existence.

Christ consciousness is an important concept to grasp if we are to understand the heart of Cayce's teachings. But it is also a phrase that, coupled with Cayce's frequent use of Scripture, could throw us off the track if we allow ourselves to think of it as an endorsement only of New Testament theology.

As a Sunday school teacher, Cayce drew heavily on all the truths of the Bible, those found in Old and New

Testament alike. Because he believed deeply in both traditions, he obviously regarded conflicts between Judaism and Christianity to be false and unnecessary. Moreover, the Judeo-Christian tradition itself has no monopoly on the principles taught by Jesus. The Buddha and other masters have voiced them as well.

Over the millennia the principles of Jesus have been hindered by being tied to religious and geopolitical controversies. But really these principles don't need to be defended so much as they need to be practiced. What if we actually did love our enemies and our neighbors as ourselves? What if we did dedicate our lives to the service of others? If we practiced kindness, patience, and love in the absence of rancor, as Cayce often suggests we should? In other words, what if we did put the Golden Rule at the top of our priorities as Jesus suggested?

The fact is, this principle is expressly common to most of the religions of the world, if in slightly different wordings. Cayce's ecumenicalism is a reflection of the universality of this teaching. And it is just this ecumenicalism that frees us to evaluate Cayce's words—and those of Jesus—for their own sake, regardless of our own religious backgrounds. For in point of fact, these teachings are both the result of and ways to further growth of the Christ consciousness.

Christ consciousness, though, is more than—and yet simpler than—the Golden Rule. As Cayce uses the term, it refers to an awareness that exists within each of us, whether we are conscious of it or not, that we are part of the oneness of the Creative Forces, of God. This knowledge is unconscious in most of us but can be brought to consciousness. We can open ourselves, can attune ourselves, to these forces. This attunement leads to a greater alignment of an individual's will with the will of God, with the will of the Creative Forces. Such an alignment in turn leads to a new way of viewing the world, a new way of living in the world, a new way of relating to other people. Gradually, it leads to an ability to *use* universal forces as Jesus did.

Jesus had this consciousness completely—not just an intellectual understanding but complete attunement. It is this complete attunement to God that allowed him to be called *the Christ*. Which is why *Christ consciousness* can be used not only for Jesus but for anyone who is in the process of finding complete attunement.

Jesus as the "Way Shower"

Anyone with an inquiring mind has to accept the existence of the man Jesus as a historical fact. No single individual has had as much impact on human history. Think about it: Would the calendar used throughout most of the world have been based on the birthdate of a myth?

For Cayce, though, deciding whether Jesus' life is mythology or fact is secondary to allowing the Christ consciousness within us to permeate all our thinking. Through this step, he suggests, we can have a richer and more harmonic existence, and even reach a point where we can forgive ourselves. This is why Cayce regards Jesus as the "way shower," the supreme guide who points out the most reliable way for everyone to blend with the Universal Forces. Jesus, he feels, brought God to the material plane to make the spirit of God more approachable for us all.

Here's how Cayce expressed this notion in reading number 1158-14, citing words from Scripture: "For as has been given, 'As thy spirit beareth witness with my spirit,' ye KNOW thyself to be children of the living God; begotten, as of love, through the Son, made manifest in flesh. Not as aliens but as brethren, as those that are heirs—yea, joint heirs with the Christ who manifested, as in the flesh, the infinite love of the Father that the children of men might know! One sees the infinite in the CHRIST life, one sees infinity in man's life."

From a historical point of view, I've often wondered why Jesus felt it was necessary to give up His life for the sake of the world. But *why* He did is not as important as the *impact* of what he did: showing the world the importance, the dominance, of spiritual reality over the fleeting and insubstantial world of physical matter. No thinking person can regard our flickering lifetimes on earth as substantial and permanent; they have the durability of a candle in a hurricane. No historical incident has equaled Jesus' sacrifice in dramatizing and teaching this point. Such an act of self-denial must be appreciated if only for this reason alone.

But what would happen if we had the common sense to put His teachings into action? Imagine headlines like these appearing in the papers one day:

COUNTRY A ADMITS IT SHOULD LOVE ITS ENEMIES

COUNTRY B RELUCTANTLY RESPONDS IN KIND

COUNTRY A DROPS FOOD AND MEDICINE INSTEAD OF BOMBS

COUNTRY B RESPONDS IN KIND

WORLD AWAITS IN SUSPENSE FOR RESULTS

Crazy idea? Maybe, but where are our present ideas getting us? Clearly, the world would be a lot better off—even from the point of view of enlightened self-interest—if we started putting His teachings into practice. The sad truth is, we don't do this enough. The hope is that someday we will. Nothing is blocking us but ourselves.

No wonder, then, that the teachings of Jesus echo throughout Cayce's readings. Cayce tells us just to be kind, just to be gentle, just to have patience and to love our neighbor as ourselves. Cayce's view of Christ as the divine guide and way shower reminds us that we carry the Christ consciousness within us, and that we can turn to that consciousness for spiritual help throughout our lives.

I must admit that my own struggle to understand fully the impact of Christ on our lives is far from over. Nonetheless, I can accept Cayce's suggestion that the Christ principles serve as welcome buoys as we navigate the rough waters of everyday living. In effect we are invited to turn our problems over to Him, to drop the load on His shoulders. In difficult times this can be of great help and a tremendous relief.

To summarize my understanding then: As a material expression of the divine, the Christ principles help us tune in to the Universal Forces so that we become one with them and thus assume a smoother existence. Meanwhile, Cayce's emphasis on kindness, on patience, and on unselfish service to our fellow human beings can create the optimum living conditions we all are seeking. Through the Christ consciousness residing within us, and through the teachings we have received, His spirit can be our conduit to God and the Creative Forces.

Is There a Place for God in the Modern World?

I can see how Cayce's conviction that God resides within us, that we can seek God there, would create a stabilizing effect on our lives. Access to the Creative Forces inside us would provide us with spiritual and moral guidance that can't be distorted by our surroundings. I picture this presence acting like a gyroscopic compass.

A gyroscopic compass is very different from a magnetic one. A magnetic compass can be affected by the electromagnetic distortions resulting from geographic variations; in fact, since a magnetic compass is always drawn to the pole, at the North Pole a magnetic compass is useless: it becomes so "subjective" that in a sense it can point only to itself. A gyroscopic compass, on the other hand, is unaffected by its housing or location. Unaffected, it is always able to point out the true direction.

I remember once sailing my thirty-foot sloop off Nantucket in choppy seas, when my compass suddenly went out of kilter. It was finding the North Star—the one star whose position in the night sky always remains constant—that saved the day and the hull. At the same time, it paid to look for God within to summon up the courage to face the perilous seas. Cayce tells us to look up, out, and within at the same time, for, though we can never see or touch God, we can always observe His manifestations throughout the universe, and God is the most unwavering navigational aid there is.

Still, we as believers in God don't function in a vacuum. We function in the modern world. So we must then have a sense of God as fitting in to our modern world. In considering this, I've found it helpful to look at the insights of Robert J. Jeffries, an outstanding financier, educator, scientist, and businessman who has been closely associated with the Edgar Cayce Foundation and its allied organizations, the Association for Research and Enlightenment (A.R.E.) and Atlantic University.

Jeffries points out that large numbers of people in the Western world are nowadays questioning the spiritual heritage that has been handed down through the ages. The modern mind has become restless and uncomfortable with some of the orthodox Judeo-Christian theologies. Adam and Eve, he points out with his congenial good humor, have lost their glitter. Noah and his overcrowded vessel seem distant and confusing. The virgin birth and the miracles of Jesus to some now lack credibility, as do the dogmatic teachings that are based on them. And where, after learning as much as we have about outer space, can the modern mind place heaven?

The conflict between the Bible and the documented findings of science has grown, with perhaps the most dramatic example being the battle now raging in the United States between the creationists and the secular humanists over the teaching of evolution.

In my readings, I've run across some tempering thoughts on these subjects. Emerson, for instance, defined heaven as "a state of perfect consciousness" rather than some mythical physical location in the sky—an idea compatible with Cayce's thinking. Similarly, I've come to think that maybe there need be no conflict between creationists and secular humanists.

If we accept Cayce's idea of God as the First Cause, then the theories of these two schools don't need to clash. The First Cause can be thought of as having created everything from the "big bang" on, making evolution simply a fragmentary element of Creation. In this sense I've come to think that both sides of the argument might be right, that Darwin was correct but limited. Or as my wife Elizabeth once wrote in one of her books, "The theory of evolution is only partially evolved."

Interestingly, despite the secular and scientific thrust of the twentieth century, Jeffries finds that many of us are now more intensely than ever seeking answers about the existence of God and our relationship to Him. These are fundamental questions that we increasingly feel the need to answer in the light of reason, not just through the perceived wisdom of a church. "We're looking," he notes, "for a personal and spiritual philosophy that would be both intellectually and morally acceptable on which we could base our lives."

Jeffries points out that we are examining the orthodox beliefs of our family traditions not to discard them, but to reconcile them with modern understandings; we want to find our own answers in the light of modern knowledge, which we feel can't be brushed under the rug. Jeffries adds that we can still look to theology in our own search for God, but he cautions us to be wary of the distortions of some theologians who have imposed their own self-image on fundamental truths, particularly in those schools of thought that over the years have become institutionalized.

The Bible, Jeffries reminds us, remains an imposing source for insight and personal spiritual beliefs. But science itself can also go beyond the physical to present the same spiritual values in a fresh light. Science, for instance, shows us that everything in our physical, material reality is composed of a common chemistry harmonized by immutable laws. These natural laws demonstrate that physically everything is essentially one, just as Cayce emphasizes.

In fact, science itself is now—if somewhat belatedly—exploring the spiritual dimensions of the human being. Nobel Prize winner Sir John Eccles advances the theory that the human mind is separate from the brain and, indeed, commands it. He states his experiments have demonstrated this scientifically.

The implications of a nonmaterial mind, separate from and commanding the material brain, are tremendous. By being nonmaterial, the mind would be free to roam the way Cayce's did during his readings. In fact, it would be free to survive after death since it would not be limited to the physical body. Further, it suggests the idea of an individual soul able to exist in perpetual consciousness.

Cayce spoke of the existence of this consciousness and its communion with the First Cause in reading 3188-1, when he told his questioner: "The Divine, the First Cause, is mindful of [here Cayce mentioned the name of the questioner]. This is evidenced by the very fact that the entity [the questioner] finds itself conscious of being itself and aware of good and evil, light and darkness, life and death. These are all one . . . there is no death to the spiritual."

Human consciousness, says Robert Jeffries, as well as

the human conscience, can be regarded as divinity manifested. That there clearly is more to human beings than the mere physical is not only evidence to Jeffries that God exists, it is the basis for his belief in the spiritual nature of God.

Meditation: One Route to the Divine

In trying to answer our first question, "Is there a God?", we are forced to explore the infinite with a limited and finite mind. It's like trying to describe an entire house by squinting through a keyhole, or like trying to tune an FM radio station using an AM set: the wiring of the radio is just not adequate to the job. Our brain circuitry is equally limited—especially on the conscious level. Cayce's clairvoyant mind, however, has shown its capacity to break out of these limitations, as has been demonstrated in case after case of physical readings.

A similar tool is available to all of us, both in our search for God and His magnificent design for the universe, and in our attempts to apply these manifestations of God to answer life's questions and to gain insight into our problems. That tool is meditation, for which Cayce gives a simplified definition in reading 1861-19: "Meditation is listening to the Divine within." And if meditation is the act of listening to God, then prayer is the act of speaking to Him.

Edgar Cayce was hardly the first to practice meditation. The religious of Eastern and Western cultures have been practicing it for millennia. But as a modern American he was decades ahead of his time, presaging the recent wave of interest in Eastern thought and the use of meditative techniques like biofeedback for therapeutic purposes. He subscribed to the yoga techniques of disciplined deep breathing, and he believed in the importance of chakra centers within the body. Many who consulted him found great value in his suggestions to use quiet meditation for health.

More recently, the physical and mental health benefits of meditation have been attested to by George H. Hollins, Jr., M.D., a prominent New York surgeon who is on the staff of four major hospitals and is a member of the American Academy of Orthopedic Surgery. Dr. Hollins admits that he knows considerably more about medication than meditation, but he has put meditation to solid use both for himself and for his patients, and he has found rich rewards in doing so.

"One of the best mental results for ourselves and for others," Dr. Hollins wrote in the *A.R.E. Journal,* "is better control of thoughts, feelings and attitudes. Freedom from anxiety and worry is something I have experienced most of all. Why worry when you can turn over all problems to the Infinite in meditation? When we place ourselves and our loved ones and all our affairs in the hands of God we can expect all to be in divine order and for our highest good."

Coming from a busy metropolitan surgeon, those are strong words.

The Purpose of Meditation

My own religious background first exposed me to meditation through the Society of Friends, or Quakers.

They believe that God is within us as well as outside, and rests as an Inner Light and voice for us to call on and listen to directly, without the intervention of an ordained hierarchy. Cayce was not a Quaker, but his outlook was similar. Both embrace a Christianized version of the great ancient Eastern philosophies: The essence of divine energy resides in each of us.

The Quaker service consists of group meditation in silence—a silence broken by any member who feels the spirit of God has moved him to speak. Cayce sees the critical value of meditation, both alone and in groups, as a tool in our search to be at one with God. He makes it the keystone of our journey of inner discovery.

In reading 281-41 Cayce elaborates on the purpose of meditation: "Ye all find yourselves confused at times respecting from whence ye came and whither ye goeth. Ye find ourselves with bodies, with minds—not all beautiful, not all clean, not all pure in thine own sight or in thy neighbor's. And there are many who care more for the outward appearance than that which prompts the heart in its activity or in its seeking. . . ."

By then posing for the second time the question "What is meditation?" he addresses the role meditation plays in resolving this confusion: "It is not musing, not day-dreaming; but as ye find your bodies made up of the physical, mental and spiritual, it is the attuning of the mental body and the physical body to its spiritual source. . . .

"Then," he explains, "it is the attuning of the physical and mental attributes seeking to know the relationships to the Maker. THAT is true meditation."

Meditation and the Soul

It's here in reading 281-41 that Cayce speaks of the human soul in relation to meditation. For Cayce, the soul is the definitive core of every individual, where true consciousness and awareness reside. But not everyone is so certain about this. Here's how Cayce addresses these doubts:

"Many say that ye have no consciousness of having a soul—yet the very fact that ye hope, that ye have a desire for better things, the very fact that ye are able to be sorry or glad, indicates an activity of the mind that takes hold upon something that is not temporal in its nature—something that passeth not away with the last breath that is drawn but that takes hold upon the very sources of its beginning . . . the SOUL—that which was made in the image of thy Maker—not thy body, no—not thy mind, but thy SOUL was in the image of thy Creator."

I too, as you can probably guess, have been one of those doubters. All through my days of yeasty agnosticism my belief in the soul bounced back and forth like a ping pong ball in a high wind. Long before I read Cayce's helpful words, though, I had an experience that began to temper my skepticism.

A *New York Times* headline in 1967 brought me up sharply one day: "JUDGE HEARS 130 TESTIFY ON SOUL . . . MUST RULE WHICH CLAIMANT GETS PROSPECTOR'S ESTATE." This was a story I couldn't pass up.

James Kidd, it seems, had prospected part-time for gold in the ominous Superstition Mountains near Phoenix, Arizona, in the area of the legendary Lost Dutchman gold mine. As a copper miner he had never made more than three thousand dollars a year, and yet his estate, when he mysteriously disappeared back in 1949, amounted to nearly a quarter of a million dollars.

The body of James Kidd was never found, nor was his gold mine. What was found was a scrawled will in which he directed that his entire estate be given to "research for some scientific proof of a soul of the human body which leaves at death."

I was so intrigued with the story that I spent weeks on horseback in the Superstition Mountains, trying to find evidence of his body or his mine. I found neither—though the saddle sores are still with me. What I did gain, however, came as a result of the ensuing trail, the so-called Ghost Trial of the Century. Over 130 individuals, organizations, and institutions filed claims on the estate, asserting they could prove the existence of the human soul and that it left the body at death.

The estate was eventually awarded to the American Society of Psychical Research, but not until the court had heard weeks of testimony supporting the validity of telepathy, clairvoyance, and other paranormal phenomena that gave palpable evidence of life after death, demonstrating the possibility of the human soul. This was my first brush with the paranormal, and it did a lot to increase my readiness for the day when I first encountered the Cayce readings.

How Meditation Works

In numerous readings, Cayce considers the anatomy of the elements making up each individual entity: physical, mental, and spiritual. At the risk of oversimplifying a very complex scheme, we can say that Cayce viewed the inner life as divided into three basic states of consciousness: the conscious, the subconscious, and the superconscious.

It is in the superconscious that the "soul-body" resides, the one enduring spiritual essence of each individual entity; hence, it is through the superconscious that we have access to the Divine. This level of consciousness, according to the readings, was the source of Cayce's psychic information. It is also our own route to the universal knowledge we all would like to draw on as we seek attunement with the Creative Forces.

The conscious state is dedicated to the here and now; it is the level of our awareness of our own physical body and its senses. The job of the subconscious, then, is to act as a mediator between the unlimited potential of the superconscious and our finite, limited conscious state. Meditation is one method by which we can seek the soul, and through it the God that is within us.

In reading 826-11, Cayce posed his own question: "How, then, may an entity become aware of those influences of that infinite force and power...?"

The voice of the sleeping Cayce replied: "When the mental self is loosened in the quietness of those periods [meditation], when it would take cognizance of the influences about self, we find the mental as a vapor... is loosened by the opening of the self through those centers of the body that arouse the awareness of the mental to the indwelling of the spiritual self that is a portion of and encased within self. The energy... rises to the consciousness within...."

"If that mental self . . . is in accord with the Divine Will . . . there comes that consciousness, that awareness of His spirit."

Or, as one of Cayce's favorite Bible quotations puts it, "Be still and know that I am God" (Psalms 46:10).

Learning to Be Still

Meditating is not as easy as it sounds. We are reminded by Cayce that the learning process can be as awkward as a child's first attempts to walk or talk.

One of my first problems in learning to meditate was establishing a regular time and place for the fifteen minutes a day Cayce recommends as optimal—*and sticking with it*. The first thing we are supposed to do—be still—sounds simple enough, but what with the pace of modern living, coming to a dead stop can be a shock, like slamming on the brakes with a back seat full of luggage: All the cares of the day can come crashing against the back of the neck before we can duck. With my daily cares bombarding me, I have often felt restless, as if I were wasting my time.

What I found is that the very act of bringing myself to physical and mental stillness took practice. I've had to grab myself by the scruff of the neck and force myself to come to that screeching stop. A long series of deep breaths—up to twenty or thirty times—does help take my mind off my daily cares. It's well worth trying, even if the session isn't magic. The stillness itself can be creative and therapeutic.

From the practical point of view, Cayce suggests that

we sit or lie in a comfortable position, without binding clothes, and breathe deeply in the custom of yoga practice. The purpose of this is to lose the physical consciousness so that we may make contact with the universal consciousness from which creative and constructive guidance will come.

At the same time, we are to forcibly expel any grudges or unkind thoughts we bear against others. Selfish desires are to be discarded in favor of submitting the self to God's will completely. Cayce reminds us that God is near and present at all times for us to call on; essentially, we are looking to empty ourselves of all that hinders the Creative Forces from arising within us. To do this, an affirmation or prayer is helpful.

Affirmations and Ideals

Put simply, an affirmation is a sentence or two used at the beginning of a meditation to express some aspect of our relationship to the Creative Forces. It is used to focus our mind on the power greater than ourselves. Its purpose is to open up the channels in our body to this Higher Power so it can fill us and empower us. One such affirmation might be Cayce's beloved passage from the Psalms, "Be still and know that I am God."

An affirmation can be quite personal, because it is an expression of our ideal. Cayce tells us to set a spiritual ideal so as to establish what Herbert Puryear, in his book *The Edgar Cayce Primer,* called "a motivational center of gravity, a hub, or a core within." It might be something as simple as a name (Moses, Jesus, Buddha) that awakens within us a high sense of purpose. It might be a word or quality, such as *love* or *oneness*. Whatever our highest ideal might be, Cayce tells us to set it in our mind during meditation as we lessen our physical consciousness in favor of the spiritual. For as he puts it in reading 281-41: "To be absent from the body is to be present with God."

Mantras

Less often in the readings, Cayce suggests the use of mantras to help attune the vibrations of the body to the Creative Forces, just as the Eastern philosophies do.

In reading 2823-3 Cayce said: "As to the manner of meditation . . . let the mind become, as it were, attuned . . . by the humming, producing those sounds of O-O-ah-ah-umm-o-o-o; not as to become monotonous, but 'feel' the essence . . . through the body forces. . . . This will open the Kundalini forces [yogic life-forces] of the body. Then direct same to be a blessing to others. These arise from the creative center of the body itself, and as they go through the various centers direct same. . . . Surround self ever with that purpose, 'Not thy will, O God, but Thine be done, ever'—and the entity will gain vision, perception, and most of all judgment."

Cayce points out that the incantation raises all these qualities within the self and brings the self closer to the Maker within the self. He adds that it blocks selfish motives, which to Cayce is a most important condition for meditation.

Some people feel self-conscious about humming man-

tras, but Eastern history has shown their usefulness over
the centuries. I had been totally unaware of mantras until
my first encounter with them on a trek I made from
Kathmandu to the base of Mount Everest.

I'll never forget entering the darkness of a great
Buddhist monastery along one of the tortuous Himalaya
trails. Several score of monks sat cross-legged in their
burgundy robes, spines straight, heads bowed, undisturbed
by my presence. They were humming their mantras with
a rich resonance that made the timbers in the hall vibrate.
As I sat there tape recording the sounds I felt transfixed; I
could almost feel myself lifted off the ground as the
chanting went on. I realized the purpose of the mantra, of
the vibrations that arose from it. It made me aware that
all life is vibration, from the particles of the atom, to the
billions of cells within the body, to the rhythm and
pulsing of the universe itself.

The vibrations of the mantra in meditation might well
create a harmony within that helps us become attuned to
the Creative Forces, even if only a humming sound is
used. I can sense this even from the tape recording I
made years ago. If held in resonance the sound can create
physical and emotional relaxation that permits us to
become more attentive to "the still small voice that rises
within," as Cayce defines it in reading 826-11.

The late Dr. Hugh Lynn Cayce, the son of Edgar
Cayce, held doctorates in both psychology and parapsychology, and was a profound student of his father's
works. He attaches great importance to the use of
meditation in our daily lives. In reading 1861-12,
when asked, "Is it possible to meditate and obtain

needed information?'' Edgar Cayce gave out with the witty and surprising answer, ''On any subject! Whether you are going digging for fishing worms or playing a concerto!''

In summary, Hugh Lynn Cayce reminds us that meditation is the process of being still—with the focus on the release of tension, followed by relaxation, receptivity, and discovery. We should always keep in mind the paramount purpose: to unlock the higher areas of the unconscious mind; to put the self in complete alignment with the purpose of the Creative Forces.

But just in case you're thinking meditation demands never-ending solemnity, behold the welcome relief Edgar Cayce brings us in his reading 274-3: ''Then in meditation, in prayer, not in long facedness, not in closing self to those things about self that make for a contentment in the material things in life, but let those things be rather the effect and not the purpose of the mind! So may one be joyous, being kind, being loving, being open hearted. . . .''

Meditation clearly is central to the process of discovering God within us. As we explore the other important questions that follow in this book, the art of meditation will become useful to us in many more ways. For as Cayce has shown, meditation can be the most powerful vehicle for our enlightenment.

The Road I've Traveled

I'm grateful to Edgar Cayce for toppling me off the fence of my agnosticism. My position had always annoyed me because of its vacillating qualities of uncertainty and indecision. Agnosticism felt like trying to win a sports car race with the gearshift in neutral. There's something brackish about being neutral, and I try to avoid such a bland condition whenever possible. On the other hand, there can be something abrasive about passionate advocates of any belief, especially on a subject as important as God. Some well-meaning advocates feel the need to beat others over the head with their beliefs.

Cayce gives us loose reins in this matter but at the same time steers us ably. I haven't always found him easy to follow, and at times he can be intense in his convictions. But the upshot of my own exploration is that I'm now convinced of the existence of a very real, non-anthropomorphic God who plays an important and intimate role in our lives. A God of love and light whose affection is palpable. And the same is true of Cayce's conception of Jesus.

In reading 3003-1, he urges us not to look dolefully on the Christ consciousness that is within us all: "For if ye lose that ability to laugh, ye lose that ability to be joyous! . . . For remember that He laughed even on the way to Calvary; not as pictured so oft, but laughed even at those who tormented him. This is what angered them most."

The picture Cayce wants us to carry in our hearts is of a Jesus who was confident that the spiritual realm was real and indestructible. So confident was he that he laughed at the thought that the Roman soldiers, by destroying the physical body, would actually help bring the Christ principles to much of the world for generations to come, implanting them with a greater impact than if the executioners had let Him live.

At the same time, Cayce sees the thoughts of the Buddha and other masters as harmonizing with those of Jesus to enlighten the world in the ways of peace and love for our fellow creatures. In other words, no religion or school of philosophy should foster a country-club mentality that excludes nonmembers from a communion with a universal God, the Architect, the Maker, the Author, the Creator of all that exists.

QUESTION 2

What Is the Real Purpose of My Life?

Most of us are looking to make a success of our lives, and at times we're quite confident we are on the road: We feel moments of dedication, determination, and resolve. But there are other times when we feel aimless, when we grope blindly to define our goal. Is it to become a millionaire? Do we seek fame? Political power? Some other outward form of success?

A friend of mine once sought a psychiatrist's help with this question because, though he had achieved great success in business, he was feeling more unhappy and discontented than ever. He was having trouble defining true success. One answer he finally came up with was that each person must feel successful inside regardless of the opinions of others.

What we can learn from my friend's experience is that measuring up to society's common yardsticks for success—material wealth, power over others, and so on—won't necessarily answer our *inner* cravings for success. We must define what success means to us by first coming to understand the true purpose of our lives.

Caught up as we are in the rush and turmoil of everyday life, we find it hard to pursue an understanding of our true purpose. Edgar Cayce's cosmic mind was able to cut through the confusion to reach the fundamental essence, from which a true purpose could emerge into clear focus. His readings deal with the subject on all levels—the physical, the mental, and the spiritual. No single facet alone, they tell us, can create true satisfaction for the fully rounded self.

One important factor Cayce suggests we bear in mind is the distinction between ambition and fulfillment. Raw ambition seems to carry the seeds of its own destruction within it. It usually results in self-aggrandizement, which Cayce felt is a major block to true self-fulfillment.

I must admit that my own sense of purpose in life has bobbled like a yo-yo on a string. That's one reason I have looked carefully at what Cayce said about this subject.

For a long time I was content with the notion that "success" was the goal and purpose of my life—until, like my friend, I found myself having to define what success meant. A solid financial foundation and a happy home, family and good friends were of course a heavyweight chunk of what I wanted, as I'm sure they are for many others. And I still think these goals are entirely laudable. But like so many things in life, as important as they are, they are transitory, perishable.

In surveying the words of Edgar Cayce, I find he also attaches importance to these worldly goals. But what he centers on above and beyond these goals is the success of the soul, where our most intense and enduring

sense of awareness resides. He reminds us that we cannot
ignore the divine itch that simmers beneath the surface in
all of us, though we may often try to brush it away. "Not
all that is considered by some as material success," he
tells us in reading 3420-1, "is soul success."

One clear guideline is that our goals cannot be shallow,
superficial, or self-centered. There have been times in my
life when I tried to ignore this guideline, often with poor
results. But there were also times when, perhaps by
intuition, I was guided by ideas similar to Cayce's and I
have felt myself rewarded.

I once went to France to investigate an incredible
mystery. The entire population of Pont-Saint-Esprit, a
little village of three thousand souls on the banks of the
Rhône River, had gone insane on a single night.

At first the villagers noticed nothing more peculiar
than that they were struck with relentless insomnia. The
street cafés were forced to stay open all night as sleepless
villagers sought company. But within a few days, more
strange things began to happen. An enormous wave of
euphoria swept the town. People were filled with manic
hilarity and inexplicable joy; people who hadn't spoken
to one another in years embraced with loving affection.

Within a week, though, the atmosphere changed dramatically. A former army pilot jumped off the balcony of
the village hall into the crowd, screaming that he was an
airplane and could fly. Another citizen danced atop the
cables of a suspension bridge, shouting that he was a
circus performer. Children screamed that tigers walked
on their ceilings and that blood was pouring down on
them. Eventually the entire population went mad, tearing

up the village streets, until troops and the gendarmerie of a nearby town were called in to restore order.

The cause of all this madness? A shipment of moldy flour contaminated with ergot fungus had been sent to the town; their bread supply was poisoned with lysergic acid. It was the most dramatic story I have ever covered, replete with graphic, almost unbelievable scenes.

My publishers were ecstatic and gave me a substantial advance. The book became a Book-of-the-Month selection. I, needless to say, was pleased with my success— until I realized that my success sprang from the misfortunes of people who had suffered so terribly. Suddenly I felt guilty about all this money I was being paid, and I decided to send the town a large portion of my royalties. I must add, however, that I did so quite reluctantly, out of guilt, not with any sense of nobility at all.

Since that time the satisfaction I've felt from my gift has been much greater than any I would have received from the money I gave up. I feel I have been repaid many times over simply by the gratitude of those villagers. I tell this story not for self-congratulation, but as an illustration of Cayce's notion that something within us urges us to act for the good of others, and that by responding to that urge we feel rewarded.

But why is this so? What is the source of this divine itch to be selfless? And what does this itch teach us about the true purpose of our lives? Let's look at one direct answer the sleeping Cayce gave to such a question.

In reading 2795-1 a questioner asked, "What is the real purpose of my present incarnation?" Cayce's answer: "That of UNIFYING man to his oneness with that Creative Force we call God."

We shouldn't be surprised by this response—not after reading Cayce's answer to Question 1, "Is there a God?" There we learned that, while we are a part of the First Cause—God—we have become separated from him and must rejoin Him by aligning our purpose with His. In a very real sense, this could be said to be the prime purpose of anyone's life.

But why did this questioner speak in terms of "*present* incarnation"?

Reincarnation and the Soul

Many of the Cayce readings speak of reincarnation and karma—ideas that sound alien to those of us raised in the Western tradition, though in fact they are accepted by the majority of the world's population. So if we are to understand the foundations of Cayce's answer to this and other questions, we must understand his beliefs about reincarnation as well.

Cayce himself was disturbed when he first encountered the idea of reincarnation, fearing it conflicted with his deep belief in the Bible. After much study he assured himself that it did not violate Christian thought, that it was consistent with his picture of the soul on its "journey to oneness" with the Creative Forces.

More and more Westerners are opening themselves to the possibility of reincarnation these days. Many of them (Shirley MacLaine perhaps the most prominent) have been led to greater openness through exposure to Cayce's words. But my skeptical mind asked for evidence, and as usual I looked first to science.

The first chink in my skeptic's armor plating came from the work of Dr. Ian Stevenson, a psychiatrist at the University of Virginia School of Medicine who has become an astute scholar of the subject. His book, *Twenty Cases Suggestive of Reincarnation,* is a detailed study of the procedure used to select the Dalai Lama and other Tibetan lamas—a procedure based on the principles of reincarnation. The book contains masses of data, all thoroughly checked by Dr. Stevenson, that while not providing proof are certainly evidential.

But what about our inability to recall our past lives? Shouldn't we remember the experiences we've been through?

This obstacle to belief persisted in my mind until I realized its interesting parallel with the fundamentals of psychoanalysis. We have no trouble accepting that the unconscious mind, dealing only with material from our *current* lifetime, holds giant stores of information that are inaccessible to conscious memory. If memories of our current lifetime can be denied to us, why not those of past lives? Why should that be a bar to our belief?

Having come this far, I turned to the Cayce readings themselves. Cayce had already shown himself to be right about so many incredible things—his physical readings done at a distance, his recommendations for therapeutic health care—that I figured he must have some strong evidence to offer of the validity of reincarnation.

My search led me to reading 1391-1, given back in 1936. The subject of the reading was identified only as "M.S." Here's part of what Cayce said about one of M.S.'s past lives:

"The entity was then what would be termed in the

present in some organizations as a Sister Superior, or an officer as it were in those of the Essenes. . . . Hence we find the entity giving, ministering, encouraging, making for greater activities; and making for those encouraging experiences in the lives of the Disciples, coming in contact with the Master often in the ways between Bethany, Galilee, Jerusalem. For . . . the entity kept a school on the way above Emmaus on the way that goeth towards Jericho, and towards the northernmost coast from Jerusalem. The entity blessed many of those who came to know the teachings, the way, the mysteries, the understanding; for the entity had been trained in the schools of those that were of the prophets and prophetesses, and indeed the entity was indeed a prophetess in those experiences.''

In 1936, when Cayce gave his reading, not much was known about the Essenes. And yet Cayce even named specific roads and locations and incidents, many of which were totally unknown to the historians and biblical scholars of his time. But to anyone like me, not already disposed to belief in reincarnation, all this would have to sound extremely farfetched. Edgar Cayce lived more than nineteen hundred years after and many thousands of miles away from the scene. Why should I be convinced by this exotic picture of people and places?

In 1947, eleven years after Cayce spoke these words, the now-famous Dead Sea Scrolls were discovered. In 1951, four years after their discovery, excavations near the coast of the Dead Sea revealed what was thought at the time to be an old Roman fort. Now, however, this fort has been identified as the Essene monastery named Kherbet Qumran, where the Dead Sea Scrolls, we now know, were written and studied before being buried in local caves. So in fact there was an Essene monastery there.

But what about Cayce's reference to his subject, M.S.? Josephus, the Jewish historian who lived and wrote in the first century, had said that the Essene communities were made up exclusively of men—not prophetesses, not women of any kind. Cayce's reading directly contradicted the account of this ancient historian.

Following the discovery of Kherbet Qumran, graves around the monastery were opened. Here the skeletons of many women were found.

Such a case makes Cayce's views on reincarnation worthy of serious attention, even if the case can only be considered evidence, not proof.

As to proof positive—for that we may have to wait. When asked directly in reading 956-1, ''What will convince me of reincarnation?'' Cayce answered simply, ''An experience.''

Why Reincarnation?

The roots of reincarnation go back to Creation itself, a hard enough concept for any mind to grasp. The world's religions are rich with Creation myths, many of which stretch credulity to the limit. In an A.R.E. bulletin Edgar Cayce's son, Hugh Lynn Cayce, bravely undertook the task of making clear his father's conception of Creation, the soul, past lifetimes, and reincarnation, all of which are linked together.

Hugh Lynn reminds us that in Genesis, God is reported to have created man in His own image. As we learned in the answer to Question 1, "Is there a God?", this does not mean God has a body just like ours. "Only man's conceit...," Hugh Lynn wrote, "could be responsible for the anthropomorphic concept which throughout has seated God upon a throne, clothed Him in beautiful raiment, and insisted on a long white beard."

God was and always will be a spiritual being, not a physical one. And so when Genesis says God created man in His own image, that means we too were once purely of spirit. As Hugh Lynn explains, "When human beings first entered this plane, it was not in physical form. All entered as a soul, a spiritual entity, in which there was embedded a spark of the divine fire. It was man, not God, who brought into existence the physical bodies in which the soul now lodges when on earth; it was man who gradually limited himself to three-dimensional consciousness which is his present form of perception."

Having limited ourselves to this physical, three-dimensional consciousness, separating ourselves from the First Cause, it is now our task to be reunited with God, the Creative Force of which we are all a part. In reading 900-59 Edgar Cayce phrased this basic view thusly: "The whole law is to be one with the Creator yet never losing its identity for that given in the beginning, yet becoming one with the Creator... in its sojourn through the earth."

That is, the soul comes down through the ages, reincarnated through many lifetimes, and yet through all this the soul remains the ultimate consciousness of the individual. To Cayce, our sojourns here on earth create educational opportunities through which we learn the best ways to develop the soul. In reading 1227-1 he says,

"An experience through the earth's plane is for the development of the soul and not mere chance."

Before we go on, let me touch on a few points that may stick in the minds of some readers: Cayce's use of the terms "entity" and "earth," and his occasional references to astrology.

You may have noticed by now that Cayce kept referring to his correspondents as entities, not as persons. An indirect explanation of what he means by an entity arose in reading 1494-1, when a questioner asked, "Does the soul's entity change in reincarnation?"

"The soul is the entity!" the sleeping Cayce explained. "The entity is the soul and the mind and body of same. See? These only enter matter, or a new house, in incarnations."

This squares with my understanding that Cayce looked on human beings as a composite of body, mind, and soul, and that he wanted to address not only the physical person but the more important spiritual side. As he said in reading 816-3, "That there is spirit, mind and matter is self-evident . . . by the very consciousness of existence. Other individuals are . . . manifestations of their own portion of that one Creative Force." Later in the reading he adds that because only the spiritual side is everlasting, that side must be the yardstick by which we measure our life's purpose—or any other facet of life.

As to his use of the term "the earth," Cayce acknowledges in reading 5755-2 that there may be many worlds, "many universes, even much as to solar systems, greater than our own that we enjoy at present. . . . This earthly experience on this earth is a mere speck when considered even with our own solar system. Yet," he reminds us, "the soul of man, thy soul, encompasses ALL in this solar system and in others."

To those of us used to reading horoscopes in the daily paper, astrology may seem to contradict the notion that our earthly experiences are for "the development of the soul and not mere chance" as Cayce claims. The conventional view of astrology holds its influences to be predictive, dominating our lives; yet for our souls to enjoy an educational experience, the exercise of free will is essential. Cayce sees no contradiction because to him the forces of astrology are not commanding; they merely create urges or inclinations that our free will can override.

And so Cayce's general picture is this: Each soul, by its own choice, passes through many earthly sojourns and is given the chance to develop spiritually. In the process mistakes may also be made, actions may be taken that move us further away from God; but in each lifetime we are also free to act so as to make up for those errors. Each lifetime is another opportunity to move the transmigration of our soul forward through the accumulation of positive karma.

Karma and the Soul

First a word of reassurance, then one of caution.

The idea that each soul must move back and forth, from earthly sojourn to a nonphysical existence, from one reincarnation to the next, was constantly on the minds of Cayce's correspondents. From questions like the one that prompted reading 928-8, it would appear this prospect occasioned some amount of apprehension.

"Must each soul continue to be reincarnated in earth until it reaches perfection," the letter writer asked, "or are some souls lost?"

A fearsome prospect indeed. But listen to Cayce's reassuring (and almost humorous) reply: "Can God lose itself, if God be God?" A reminder that each of us, each soul, is but a part of God, and therefore, "The soul is not lost; the individuality that separated itself is lost. The reincarnation or the opportunities are continuous until the soul has of itself become an entity."

Still, that doesn't mean it's easy. One questioner, wondering about his physical development, asked, "What else is necessary for me to attain and retain physical perfection?"

Cayce's caution (reading 2982-2) states: "Perfection is not possible in a material body until you have at least entered some thirty times." And remember, this is about mere *physical* perfection. However, never one to caution his correspondents without also offering guidance and hope, Cayce pointed out, "But [you] may be able to aid the body in attaining the physical, mental and spiritual balance."

Still, many people find the idea of reincarnation frightening, particularly if they view karma as a punitive process, as if each life were a sentence of punishment for the misdeeds committed in lives before.

Cayce was pleased to reassure his questioners that, far from being punitive, the karmic process gives each individual the chance to make up for past errors in *positive* ways. He did many readings in which he told letter writers of their past lives and how they affected their current incarnation, and always this was a matter of doing right where once they had done wrong, of restoring the balance and setting their soul's course in the direction of God's plan for the universe.

This view was made clear in reading 342-2. Prompted by the question "What did I come here to do?" Cayce answered pithily, "To overcome all those things you've undone." And when asked in reading 2636-1, "For what purpose did I come into the earth at this time?" Cayce advised, "To finish many of those things ye started and didn't finish."

Karma, then, does *not* necessarily mean receiving back the treatment we gave others. It does mean having to confront one's previous activities and face the consequences, but we can do that without being subjected to retribution. For example, someone who abused people in a previous life need not come back as a person who is abused. Rather, he may dedicate his life to helping abused women and children, empathizing with their pain and sacrificing part of himself to alleviate that pain in a positive way.

In a sense this is an obligation we have to the world and to our own souls, an obligation Cayce underscored in reading 3420-1: "Then as to whether there is the development or retarding of the soul entity, is dependent on the manner in which the abilities of the entity are exercised or used."

The abilities being referred to here are those skills and inclinations that the soul entity has developed over the course of previous incarnations. And so, "Each soul enters the material experience with opportunities in the abilities that have been attained or acquired as part of the individuality and personality of the entity. Each soul entity enters with the hope of preparing itself for closer or greater communion with its First Cause.'' Later in the reading Cayce says that unless the soul entity makes the world better there is bound to be a feeling of failure.

Being of Service in the World

Many psychologists and sociologists have also claimed that our genuine happiness comes from work we do that contributes to society. In Cayce's view, by holding fast to our spiritual origin, or First Cause, we almost automatically contribute to others and in the process achieve a deep sense of satisfaction.

Anyone who has sailed into a safe harbor after weathering a violent storm knows the intense feeling of security when the mooring lines are finally snug and secure to the dock. Conversely, there is a feeling of despair if the lines won't hold and the boat is adrift. Cayce's readings tell us that the First Cause is always there for us to hold on to; that we always have a safe mooring if we seek it and hold on to it, since no finite storm has the power to destroy it.

As a sailor, I've brought my boat into scores of marinas and can't recall a time when a helping hand wasn't available. Any good seaman is always ready to jump from his boat to help an incoming vessel that needs mooring. This spirit of camaraderie is contagious; it's an unwritten law of seamanship that raises the spirit within— not just of the person being helped but of the helper as well. This is an illustration of Cayce's thought that real satisfaction comes from helping others.

The goal of helping others, of course, is far greater than a mere feeling of satisfaction. As Cayce phrases it in one of his poetic metaphors, we will enter heaven leaning on the arm of someone we have helped. But that desire for satisfaction—or, for that matter, the sense of lacking satisfaction—is an invaluable reminder of the importance of knowing the purpose of your life.

Cayce, you may remember from Question 1, is persuaded that the soul resides in that area of consciousness he calls the superconscious. It is there that a lack of purpose is felt to fester as a vague and unidentified need for us to fulfill. In other words, we all have a deep desire to make the world a better place to live in, a desire to help our fellow beings, to harmonize with the Creative Forces and join them—whether or not we are fully aware of the true source of that desire. That urge, that itch, is, as the readings explain it, the desire of our soul to reach perfection in its travels toward reunification with God. Perhaps this is why, in reading 3420-1, Cayce suggests we keep a strong call to service as an ideal.

Setting an Ideal

In Question 1 we learned how important setting an ideal is in the practice of meditation. A spiritual ideal serves, in Herbert Puryear's words, as "a motivational center of gravity, a hub, or a core within." Whether it is a single word or name, or some more complicated concept, it serves to awaken within us a high sense of purpose.

Likewise, we must also set an ideal for our purpose in life, Cayce admonishes. If we don't, we are like a kayaker shooting the rapids without a steering paddle. Setting an ideal is vital to keeping us on course as our soul seeks growth through our deeds. As he told his questioner in reading 816-3, when asked the purpose of an entity's material manifestation, "An entity's experience in...material manifestation is to make the path straight. For today in the experience of every soul is the opportunity to make manifested that which is ideal in the experience of that entity."

I will confess that in attempting to apply Cayce's principles to my own use, I sometimes have trouble understanding the setting of an ideal as the basis for my purpose in life. But that Cayce considered it of paramount importance is clear from many of his readings. And I am heartened by what seems to be a promise, again from reading 816-3, that if we measure our lives against the yardstick of our ideal, and if we strive to be patient and tolerant with our fellow beings so that they find fresh hope from our example, we will continue to grow in spiritual development and understand our purpose in a clearer light.

Our Highest Service

It is in this expectation—that our fellow beings may find fresh hope from our example of patience and tolerance—

that Cayce hints at what may be our highest service, the most powerful help we can be to others.

Over and over in the readings he stresses that we should carry our sense of purpose beyond ourselves to illuminate others with the same ideas. He reminds us in reading 2272-1 that we have an opportunity to be a "living example known and seen by those whom we might meet of the fact that God IS." Cayce adds, "Those who live in their associations with others as to make others more aware of Him . . . are fulfilling the purpose for which an individual experience is given."

It's refreshing that Cayce doesn't recommend great missionary zeal but rather that we demonstrate by example. His reading 877-1 points out that our individual purpose as an entity is unique, but always in the sense of being companions and co-creators with God.

The goal of helping others to move closer to attunement with the Creative Forces also helps explain what might otherwise seem like a paradox. The clarification comes in reading 275-39: "That which is so hard to be understood in the minds and experiences of many is that the activities of the soul are for self-development, yet must be selfless in its activities for . . . the soul to develop."

Cayce reminds us further that Jesus said, "I of myself can do nothing. The Father worketh in me. He doeth the works that you see." In this way we are reminded to draw on the Creative Forces to give to others, and thereby reduce our own separation from that celestial mooring we strive for.

And so, conveniently, we have a convergence of purposes here: As we seek to attune ourselves to the universal design of the Creative Forces, as we seek our own alignment with God, the First Cause, we may foster our soul's perfection by bearing witness to others that God is—and we don't have to go out of our way to do it. We simply have to demonstrate it in our treatment of our fellow beings. As Cayce says in reading 641-6:

"Know first the ideal—not merely of a spiritual nature, but of a mental and material also. Not so much as ye would desire that others be, or that others might do for thee, but rather as to whether or not thy material or daily activity in dealing with thy fellow men is in keeping with thy spiritual ideal. . . . Is there stress laid upon the ideal . . . that as you would have others be, that ye be thyself?"

He continues by underscoring that it is through our treatment of others, guided by our ideal, that spiritual growth is attained: "Thus we find that the ideal from the spiritual angle, as well as the mental and material, becomes not merely as a tenet, but as a practical, living thing in the experience of the entity, and thus does growth come."

The "rule" implied here is the fundamental one for most of the world's great religions: the Golden Rule. It can serve as an "ideal" ideal, the one we should keep foremost in mind at all times, as a navigational fix.

The reading then summarizes Cayce's guidance about knowing and achieving life's purpose: "Know that the purpose for which each soul enters a material experience is that it may be a light unto others. . . ." And he encourages us along that path by promising, "Life and its problems become not a burden, but opportunities for the greater expressions and expansions of self in knowing that as ye sow the daily fruit of the spirit ye need not worry and fret thyself as to its growth." For that reason, and because the search for God is paramount, we should "be not weary in well-doing."

Reaping Our Rewards

For those of us used to setting and pursuing goals more traditionally, then, Cayce's perspective is quite new, for we are encouraged to approach our goals indirectly. But if this strikes you as disappointing in terms of achieving material goals and well-being, it shouldn't. Cayce was convinced that approaching our goals through unselfish service to others will bring not only true soul satisfaction but the enjoyment of material rewards in many surprising ways.

Boiled down, his words tell us that if we approach finite and limited goals indirectly, always guiding our actions by our journey to oneness with God, as part of our exploration of our own Christ consciousness, the more material objectives not only will follow, but will become more enriched and less transitory; we will enjoy them more because our daily contact with the real purpose of our life will have made us fuller, more well-rounded beings.

As to our ultimate reward, the rejoining of our soul with God the Creator, I am left picturing a soul eager to reach a state of peace with itself, a soul anxious to take advantage of each earthly sojourn so as to hustle along its development, and perhaps a soul that is a little impatient to finally end this cycle and return home.

When asked by a questioner in reading 295-2, "Will it

be necessary to re-enter this earth plane?'' Cayce gave
the only counsel possible:

"So live so act in the present, that it will not be
necessary.''

QUESTION 3

How Can I Find Peace in a Turbulent World?

I'm struck by a television commercial promoting relaxed vacations in Florida: A waitress stands on the terrace of a posh hotel and invites the viewers to "come on down" to Florida and forget the cares of the day. "We won't even allow you to read today's newspaper," she says.

Here's a vivid illustration of how we are bombarded on a daily basis with the turmoil of our turbulent world. News stories of political upheavals, bloody uprisings, and strife can't help but create within us a feeling of personal distress, a feeling that we are being tossed about by events fully out of our own control. Faced with epidemics, natural disasters, and widespread crime, we are bound to feel vulnerable, helpless, sometimes even hopeless.

Particularly distressing is the sight of man's inhumanity to man: the constant reports of serial murders, rape, and cruelty that flash across our TV screens; the newspaper accounts of bloodshed and repression, of massive starvation when famine relief is blocked for political and military reasons.

Most frustrating is that, to the eyes of the average person, there is nothing we can do to correct the situation. All we can do is accept it. Faced with events like these, though, it can be as hard to accept the condition of the world as it was for Margaret Fuller to "accept the universe."

That famous old poem by Rudyard Kipling, called "If," suggests that if you can keep your head when everything around you is basically going nuts, you deserve a good pat on the back. Now, I've always considered this an extremely soupy, sloppy, and sentimental poem. But it does get its point across.

This brings up a tricky problem we must deal with when we explore any striving for higher goals of the spirit. It's a problem I've run into in writing this book. There's a narrow tightrope I must walk in distinguishing between mawkish sentimentality and genuine reverence; between a "goody-goody" syndrome and deep spiritual awareness. That's why I respond so to the answer Edgar Cayce gave when a letter writer asked if it's possible to get "needed information" through meditation. Cayce's reply, that meditation is good for anything from finding fishing worms to playing a concerto, is an example of the salty wit with which he avoids sentimentality and keeps his guidance accessible to everyone. In fact, I find that throughout his works Cayce always manages to keep one foot on the ground, even while he often soars to exalted heights.

This attitude is of special importance for the question we are considering here: how to find peace in a turbulent

world. It's helpful to remember that Cayce's guidance—
that we learn to blend our will with God's will—has a
solid, practical application when our head is spinning
from the chaos of the world around us. With the forces of
the world making us feel tossed like paper cups in a
windstorm, we are forced to rely on our inner resources
more than ever before; by keeping Cayce's main principle
in mind, by remembering that the Creative Forces exist
both within us and outside us, we have a source to draw
on for energy, strength, and power in unlimited quantity.
In that way we can bolster our courage and spirits and
keep our balance on life's tightrope.

Most of us are familiar with the advice contained in a
prayer that goes under more than one name: the Mother's
Prayer, the Serenity Prayer, and probably several others.
It asks for the strength we need to change the things we
can change, the serenity to accept the things we can't
change, and the wisdom to know the difference between
the two. An excellent thing to pray for, and excellent
advice as far as it goes; but what it doesn't tell us is how.

And so let's look at some of Edgar Cayce's psychic
readings to see what advice they offer in the pursuit of
the ever-important hows: how we can achieve our own
inner peace and stability amid such turbulence, and how
we can carry the message of peacefulness to the world in
a meaningful and effective way.

Stand By Your Ideal

For reasons we'll discuss more fully later in this
chapter, the Cayce readings tell us that any individual

hoping to move the world toward a more peaceful state must first achieve his or her own inner peace. Only by achieving true inner peace can you be a light of peace to others. As we've seen, however, achieving inner peace seems no simple matter; in a modern life so filled with doubt and strife, in a world where truth itself *appears* to be relative, what we hunger for is some rock to hold on to, some anchor to give us spiritual stability.

One first step, according to reading 1977–1, is to learn to "consider life as a whole" for peace and harmony to be present. "It is not all of life to live," Cayce explains, "nor . . . all of death to die. For life and death are one, and only those who will consider the experience as one may come to understand or comprehend what peace indeed means."

While at first blush this might seem nothing but a little hand-holding, a reassuring suggestion that you not be afraid of death because death and life are one, it is more. It is a reminder to keep in mind the true purpose of your life, the goal of each individual to locate the divine within him and attune himself to those Creative Forces, in deed as well as in thought. In this way, Cayce says, "ye shall live in peace" because you are living "in harmony with God's laws."

Living in accordance with God's laws, the reading tells us, provides not just inner harmony but harmonious relationships with those with whom we share our planet: "Know that just as ye are a part of a family, ye are part of a city, a part of the law, a part of the country, a part of the universe."

And if we don't? Cayce tells us to consider the outcome carefully: "Then what will thy harvest be if ye only sow . . . seeds of selfishness . . . without regards [for] the thoughts and purposes of others?'' The answer is one we have heard throughout the ages, that ''whatsoever a man soweth, that must he also reap.''

But knowing—and holding on to—the true purpose of your life isn't automatic either. The guidance discussed in Question 2, ''What is the real purpose of my life?'', applies here as well: ''Know first your ideal in spiritual things,'' we are told in reading 3128–1. ''Choose that which is thy pattern.'' For it is by knowing your spiritual ideal and applying it in your daily work that you ''can contribute the most . . . in a happy, peaceful, satisfying manner that brings the peace of Him who IS the light of the world.''

Remain faithful to your spiritual ideal, Cayce tells us. This is what can serve as your stabilizing anchor. Even if external circumstances are chaotic and threatening, be faithful to your ideal. Even if your material rewards or social status suffers, be faithful to your ideal. ''To be sure, there are floods in the life,'' the reading acknowledges, ''there are dark days and there are days of sunshine. But the soul-entity stayed in a purpose that is creative . . . may find the haven of peace.'' Because, reading 1977–1 tells us, if what you sow is your ideal, then ''that alone [your ideal] may ye reap in thy experience.''

Know Whom You Glorify

One corollary—perhaps a prerequisite—as well as an outgrowth of knowing your spiritual ideal and living by it is knowing whom your actions are meant to glorify: yourself or God.

The doing of good works is always important. But if your life choices, even though helpful to others, are made for the purpose of self-aggrandizement, true peace will not be the result.

A soul "finds himself a co-creator with the Divine that is manifested in self," reading 622–6 reminds us. "Thus, if the choice leads the entity into the exalting of self, it becomes naught in the end. [But] if the choice is that self is to be used . . . to GLORIFY the Creative Force, then the body, the mind, finds that peace, that harmony, that PURPOSE for which it chose to enter a material experience." That is, peace will be ours only if we are attentive to our motivations, if we remember that our actions should be guided by our desire to unite with the Creative Force within us and do its will, not for personal status and acclaim.

With this linking of the ideal, the nature of God, and the true purpose of an individual's life—a linking familiar to us from Cayce's answers to "Is there a God?" and "What is the real purpose of my life?"—it is no surprise that Cayce should summarize in reading 256–4: "In this manner of consecration of self, self's abilities, in service to Him, may there come that joy, that peace, in that service." For if we are always aware that our service to the world is part of our effort to align our will with the will of God, then we are working toward our prime purpose in life—rejoining with the Creative Force—and that, says Cayce, will bring us peace.

A similar thought is expressed in reading 136–2, where we are told to "establish that One-ness wherein the inner self . . . beareth witness with His spirit.'' What we are urged to seek is a very subjective feeling that our will is at one with God's will, that our life is being lived in accordance with God's desire for it—a sense that we are a part of the energy that is God and that, because we are a part of it, we are expressing it through our life.

The routes to this subjective sense of oneness are meditation and living: meditation because it is a uniquely helpful tool for coming into visceral contact with the God within us, and living because it is through the conduct of our life that we may fulfill the purpose of our present incarnation. Living ''not for self-indulgence, not for self-glory, not for self-aggrandizement; for these only bring heartaches as well as turmoil and strife,'' says reading 622–4. Rather, living in a way that establishes our oneness with God, for ''peace is the longing of the soul, and to be at-onement with Creative Forces alone may bring peace in the consciousness of any.''

Trust and Take Risks

''Put away those things that would cause fear and doubt,'' advises reading 262–128. Abide in God day by day.

Fundamentally, we are being reminded that peace comes through trusting in God and abiding in His word. But really this is more than simple advice to listen to God. It is a challenge. We are being told to live a life of faithfulness even in the face of things that would cause fear and doubt; that is, to live according to the will of the Creative Forces regardless of how difficult that makes things. Even when others threaten us, we must be willing to take whatever risks God is calling us to take.

As is most apparent, this means not renouncing our spiritual convictions, standing firm in our beliefs. More than that, though, we are told to overcome *any* fear in order to live for God. Since that means living in accordance with the will of the Creative Forces, that means standing up for what is right in *any* area. And not just now and then but, as Cayce says, "in His way ye abide day by day"—every day of our life.

No, It's Not Easy

If achieving peace requires we have the courage of our convictions, it also requires an unrelenting consistency. It's not enough, apparently, to say our prayers and attend religious services. "Think not that there is any short cut to peace or harmony," says reading 1901-1, "save in correct living." We can't abide by God's word only on the Sabbath and in our charity work, yet suspend our convictions, our ideals, in our other dealings. Cayce's warning is clear and, when you think about it, logical: "Ye CANNOT go against thine own conscience and be at peace with thyself, thy home, thy neighbor, thy God!" The reason, according to Cayce, goes back to his basic principle: just as each of us is but the material manifestation of the Creative Force in a material world, so too is every one of our fellows a part of God, and hence, "As ye do unto the least of thy brethren, ye do it unto thy Maker." However poorly you treat your neighbor, that is how you are treating God. That, says Cayce, is something your conscience can never live with peacefully.

Not is it enough, Cayce tells us in reading 524-2, to live out our ideal through the doing of so-called good works. The commandment to "love the Lord thy God with all thine heart, thine soul, thine body" doesn't stop there; it adds: "and thy neighbor as thyself." We must use every opportunity to live out our spiritual ideal, not just in charitable endeavors, not just in our life's major projects, but "in the home, in the street, in the market place, or in associations with the individuals in their various walks of life." These are the "channels," the opportunities we have to apply this commandment. In return, we are promised, "the soul, the heart, the mind may grow in grace, in knowledge, in understanding, and thus create . . . first contentment, then peace and harmony."

Hide Not the Light

"Make . . . peace with thine *own* inner conscience," Cayce told a questioner in reading 165-22. "Then hide not the light under a bushel."

This advice seems to lie at the heart of Cayce's counsel that we achieve peace through our relationships with other people. Our own behavior should serve as an example of "a life well lived and in service to others" —which demands a lot more than just remembering to say, "Have a nice day!" It requires, according to reading 1901-1, that we exercise our abilities—really *use* ourselves— in a way that will bring "hope and cheer and patience and love and harmony in the lives of all [we] touch."

It's here that the notion of Christ consciousness becomes a very practical matter. You'll remember from
Question 1 Cayce's teaching that the Christ consciousness—
the awareness that we are part of the oneness of the
Creative Forces—resides in all of us whether we are fully
conscious of it or not. Jesus, because He was attuned to
this consciousness completely, lived his life in complete
accord with it, demonstrating it to all around him through
his actions.

Cayce, in his readings, holds up Jesus' life as an
example of how we may achieve peace by spreading
peace—spreading it by demonstrating to those around us
behavior that is true to the Creative Forces' plan for the
universe. In reading 272–7 Cayce reminds us that "the
way has been shown by His Son in the earth. 'He went
about doing good' day by day. Not any great revelation,
not in the fanfare of trumpet, not in segregating self from
the world; . . . rather that the world *through* Him might
know more of the Father's love for those in this material
plane." That is, Jesus acted not for his own glory but for
the purpose of showing the world God's love—something
nobody can do if they cloister themselves and stay aloof
from the world.

Cayce tells us that we are Jesus' brothers and sisters,
that we are all true "children of Light," and so we
should do as Jesus did day by day. "A kindness shown
here, a gentleness shown there, no harsh words to those
that falter. . . ." By setting such an example, those around
us will learn "to speak gently, even to an erring son,"
and then they too will carry the message onward to
others.

Our reward for following this path, for allowing "the

shining light of His love" to pass on to "those that ye meet—yea, in the street, in the home, . . . in the throng," is strength, hope, and peace.

One of the qualities Cayce suggests we demonstrate (reading 1326–1) is patience. "Others may do as they may," he bids us say, "but as for me—I will serve a living God. I will manifest patience . . . brotherly love."

I find it interesting that he uses the word "manifest." He does, I imagine, because he means us to be making manifest in the world qualities that flow from the nature of the Creative Forces. In his view we are doing more than setting an example; we are being a "co-creator with God" by bringing forces to bear in the world that further God's plan. That is why the prediction in this reading states: "If ye would have peace, be peaceable. If ye would have friends, show thyself friendly. If ye would be loved, be lovely to those ye know."

Again, this is not an easy assignment, for Cayce wants us to be "lovely" not only to those who are open to loveliness, but even "to thy enemies, to those that despitefully use you; for in thus doing ye may find that happiness, those promises as thy very own." Here's another example of the risks Cayce says we must take; turning the other cheek, greeting ill will with patience, will always feel like a risk. The reward he promises, though, is not only the inner peace we gain from knowing we are doing God's will, but an increased store of goodwill in the world from which we all will benefit.

It's Okay to Be Human, Too

If all of this makes you fear you're not up to the job; if, as I do, you worry that only a saint could be this perfect, Cayce has reassurances for you, too. You don't need to *be* perfect to carry this message to others. All you have to do is strive for it.

A good example is the reading Cayce gave for a woman back in 1934. According to the words he spoke while in an altered state of consciousness, this woman was hardly viewed as a saint by everyone around her. And yet, says reading 516–2, "While oft there has been criticism of the actions of the entity in its associations, in its relations with individuals and with groups," there were those who blessed her for the renewed hope they gained from her activities. Many people have sought in vain, Cayce said, for the source of this renewed hope, this outlook upon life. What they did not find is that "it has been the *undercurrent* from the activities of this entity; and peace has come into the inner soul of the entity from these very activities."

It's a great relief to know, then, that we are permitted to be human. I can't imagine never feeling anger, jealousy, or hatred. But according to reading 476–1 we need not expect automatic perfection from ourselves. We need not deny the reality of these emotions. What we should do is acknowledge that they exist and then work to transform them into their opposites—forgiveness, love, and caring. "These very influences *spiritualized*," the reading says, "may make for soul development, even though it passes through hardships, that will bring peace, happiness, joy, harmony. Are not these the opposite of hate, malice and contention?''

My Affirmations

The sleeping Edgar Cayce, we now see, gave much useful instruction to the serious seeker of inner peace, and all of it based on his fundamental principle: that our lives should be lived in a way that helps us rejoin the Creative Force by aligning our will with God's. Accomplishing that takes work, it seems to me; but more than that, I find I need help keeping my ideal in mind.

Cayce considered the Lord's Prayer to be the perfect affirmation to use for this purpose. But I've found that merely repeating it by rote is not effective; I need to clarify every line, search out its application in practical living, as I go through it. Important implications come alive for me when I apply my intellect to it line by line. For instance:

"Our Father who art in heaven..." By putting the emphasis on the "Our," I'm reminded that I am not staking out a request merely on my own behalf but for everyone else in the world—all of whom have just as much right to address Him as I do. Also, I find it important when I say this line to think of heaven according to the definition "a perfect state of consciousness." That way I am not bogged down by images that don't make sense for me; I can imagine instead a state of awareness where a nonanthropomorphic God might abide.

Continuing with the prayer: "Hallowed be *Thy* name..." puts the emphasis on Him, on my hope to put the burden of the world's turbulence on Him, who has the strength to handle it, and who has a purpose we may not be able to discern with our limited, finite sight.

Next: "*Thy* kingdom come, *Thy* will be done . . ." With this emphasis I am not asking for personal favors but for my own acceptance of the ultimate design of the universe, which is also beyond the ken of my limited vision. What appears to me to be senseless turmoil may only be the ugly scaffolding needed to complete His brilliant architectural design.

As the prayer concludes, there could be other emphases to suggest that the Infinite Power is steering the world capably in spite of its apparent chaos. Suppose the emphasis were to be, "For Thine is the *real* kingdom, the *real* power, the *real* glory, forever. Amen." We might even substitute the word "only" for "real" here to suggest that our despair about the condition of the world might be the result of our failure to tune in to God's infinite, long-range view.

Another approach to understanding—and truly applying—the Lord's Prayer comes from A.R.E. staffer Mark Thurston. He suggested to A.R.E. study groups that they rephrase the prayer in modern terms in order to better utilize it in the modern world. I find that, though the lyrical poetry is lost in the rephrasing, the modernizing has helped me to apply the great basic principles to current life. I close this chapter by offering it to you, in the hope that you can use it in your own search for peace.

To the Creative Force that has put all of us here:
Your power is above all of ours.
Help us join in your unseen harmony.

Help us to put your design ahead of ours in our
limited, as opposed to your infinite, sight.

Give us the courage and intelligence to meet our needs.

Forgive us the injustices we do to others.

Help us to avoid distraction and deliver us from the
destructive forces within and outside ourselves.

For the world of total reality is yours, not ours;

Whatever power we have comes from you, that is the
source of all our accomplishments.

Amen.

QUESTION 4

How Can I Acquire My Best Health and Highest Energies?

Because the startling career of Edgar Cayce began with his medical healings, it's not surprising that considerable attention has been paid over the years to what he said about maintaining physical health and about curing illness. While most of these psychic health readings were in response to individual requests, many of them still contain advice that can be put to general use. As a result, laymen and medical scientists alike have combed the archives compiled by the A.R.E. and the Edgar Cayce Institute in Virginia Beach, both as a rich resource for research and for practical application.

Among the findings of Edgar Cayce are his views on self-healing, diet, exercise, and folk medicine, including many methods that have proved safe and simple and yet are equal to or better than the more sophisticated pharmaceuticals that make up the physician's standard armamentarium.

I should point out that both of these Cayce institutions, aware that the psychic readings were meant to apply to specific cases for the most part, are careful to recommend that these medical measures be attempted only with the cooperation of a health-care professional—particularly one acquainted with the Cayce methods. In addition, these procedures are the sort that should be practiced with over-the-counter remedies.

How It Works

Cayce's medical teachings can all be said to rest on a central principle, one that should sound familiar to us from the understanding of human dimensions we learned in Question 1: "The spirit is the life, the mind is the builder, the physical is the result." To Cayce, health and healing embrace mental and spiritual elements at least as much as any physical treatments. If this sounds commonplace to us today, we must remember that Cayce did his work long before the importance of psychosomatic medicine was fully recognized and dealt with. He was, then, the forerunner of holistic healing, now an integral arm of medical practice.

For example, pointing out the importance of mental serenity to good health, Cayce says in reading 3510–1, "For anger can destroy the brain as well as any disease. For it is itself a disease of the mind." And in reading 470–37 he advises, "Don't get mad and don't cuss a body out, mentally or in voice. This brings more poisons than may be created by even taking foods that aren't good."

Nor is it just our attitudes toward ourselves and our own bodies that can affect our health; in reading 4021–1

Cayce warns us against bearing a negative attitude toward the world and the people around us: "To be sure attitudes oft influence the physical conditions of the body. No one can hate his neighbor and not have stomach or liver trouble. No one can be jealous and allow the anger of same and not have upset digestion or heart disorder."

Unlike traditional psychosomatic medicine, though, Cayce also focused on the important role played by the spiritual element. This carries holistics beyond the mental, way beyond the five senses. But for Cayce, this should be no block to our own participation; he was convinced that everyone is not only psychic but can apply the power of the unconscious mind directly to health and energy patterns.

Cayce firmly held the view that all force, all power, emanates from the One Force of our Maker, but he also knew that the health and energy emanating from that source may be properly applied or may be misdirected. Because a human being is made up of several states of consciousness—the mental, the spiritual, and the physical—all these states must be harmonized, harnessed, and directed to achieve the health and energy we need. After all, don't most physicians frankly admit that it is not they who do the healing? It is the patient's own body and mind that do so.

For those of us who insist on a more detailed, material explanation (Cayce knew there'd be those who would demand it), he offered the following explanations in reading 281–3: "Let's analyze healing for the moment, to those that must . . . see a material demonstration, occasionally at least!

"Each atomic force of a physical body is made up of . . . positive and negative forces that brings it into a material plane. These . . . being electrical in nature as they enter into material basis or become matter in [their] ability to take on or throw off. So, as a group may raise the atomic vibrations that make for those positive forces [that] bring divine forces in action in a material plane, those [forces] that are destructive are broken down by the raising of that vibration! That's material, see? This is done through Creative Forces, which are God in manifestation!

"Hence as self brings those little things necessary . . . for position, posture, time, period, place, name, understanding, study each and assist each in their respective sphere. So does the entity become the healer."

The Healing Power of Groups

Cayce was a stout advocate of group efforts in healing: individuals joined together for mutual aid and comfort, certainly, but also for the enhancement of the healing process itself. For, just as spreading the Christ consciousness can spread peace, so too can the Christ consciousness have a profound effect on all who participate in such an effort. For each individual in the group, he advised, "there must be raised in each . . . the superseding of the Christ consciousness in that matter would be healed."

It is through attunement to the Christ consciousness, he suggests, that we may overcome the ills the flesh has become heir to as a result of entering into the material world. To accomplish that, cooperation within the group must raise the vibrations not only in the self who is ill but in the others involved, which means avoiding self-centeredness in order to raise the consciousness of all. If there is doubt and fear, Cayce advises us to "close the senses to the material things and to lose the self in Him."

What this reminds me of is the importance of belief to this—indeed, to any—healing process. When one correspondent wrote to ask if she could heal a friend, Cayce reminded her that she first had to persuade the friend to develop a sincere desire to be healed, which can only come from within the self.

The Credibility Factor

Credibility and trust are essential to any healing relationship. Our first concern when we look for a new doctor, for example, is whether we think we can trust him or her. So too, I find, with Cayce's teachings: credibility is critical to accepting that his recommendations are worth following. That's why, in making up my own mind, I looked first at literature showing how Cayce's teachings were used by medical practitioners. And the more I dug, the more the credibility factor was supported.

Healing the Sick

Cayce, of course, had recommendations for maintaining good health as well as for curing illness. Let's look first, though, at how some of his teachings were used in treating disease, a fruitful area to turn to when seeking dramatically convincing evidence.

One of the many health professionals who helped spread Cayce's healing prowess was the late Dr. Harold J. Reilly. A physiotherapist by training, he coordinated his work with many prominent New York physicians and, along with Ms. Ruth Hagy Brod, wrote *The Edgar Cayce Handbook for Health through Drugless Therapy*. The book recounts Reilly's many successful experiences applying the Cayce principles to the healing of his clients, which eventually included a long list of corporate tycoons, movie stars, and union and political leaders such as New York's Governor Nelson Rockefeller, George Meany, John L. Lewis, Gloria Swanson, and David Sarnoff.

Dr. Reilly first encountered the work of Edgar Cayce when a woman walked into his office and presented him with a transcribed psychic reading of her physical condition. The reading claimed she was suffering a toxic condition brought about by emotional disturbance, poor circulation, and improper elimination.

When Reilly heard that Cayce had diagnosed the woman while in a trance, he was sure his leg was being pulled. Nonetheless, the recommended treatments corrected her problems with startling success, and so began a team effort involving Cayce, Reilly, and the doctors Reilly worked with that lasted until Cayce's death in 1945. (Actually, the combined effort went on long beyond that time because the readings in the archives continued to help Dr. Reilly provide better health and well-being for his clients; like many other Cayce advocates, Dr. Reilly found the readings to be "living things" that kept Cayce's influence alive.)

Reilly, a down-to-earth pragmatist, was impressed that Cayce's format for health brought a sense of urgency to maintaining good circulation and to eliminating all we take in. The emphasis here was on diet rather than on laxatives (Cayce urged drinking six to eight glasses of water a day to flush the system), plus exercise and massage for proper circulation and body tone. As a physiotherapist, Reilly was delighted to hear recommendations like those.

Cayce's recommendations for spinal adjustments, physiotherapy, and osteopathic treatment began with those first cases of his that startled the medical establishment, and continued throughout his life's work. Dr. Reilly had shunned a degree in osteopathy, choosing instead to study physiotherapy, mainly because he wanted to work closely with conventional medical doctors, who at the time were more willing to refer their patients to therapists than to osteopaths. That same problem still remains today: osteopaths and chiropractors are often viewed skeptically by mainstream doctors. Yet Cayce was adamant that there were virtues to both disciplines, especially when it came to preventive measures in the pursuit of health.

In his reading 902–1 Cayce directly addressed his support of osteopathy this way: "As a system of treating human ills osteopathy. . . is more beneficial than most measures that may be given. Why? In any preventative or curative measure, that condition to be produced is to assist the system to gain its normal equilibrium. It is known that each organ receives impulses from other portions of the system by the suggestive forces. [He is referring here to the sympathetic nervous system, and later to the cerebrospinal system and blood supply.] These course through the system in very close parallel activity in every single portion of the body." He concludes by adding that the stimulation of the ganglia is bound to be helpful to the equilibrium of the body.

It was not only as a pragmatic physiotherapist, however, that Reilly found himself in agreement with Cayce. He eventually came to believe as strongly as Cayce did in relying on Divine energy as a critical part of achieving true health. Reilly singled out reading 5439 as an ideal for physical well-being: "For the body physical is truly the Temple through which the mental and the spiritual and soul development must manifest, and in manifestation does the growth come."

In his book, Dr. Reilly talks of how carefully he pondered this Cayce phrase, deciding eventually that it perfectly reflected his own deep beliefs. He also agreed with Cayce that fear and hatred are the greatest enemies of robust health and vitality. In sum, over his long years of incorporating the Cayce methods into his practice, Dr. Reilly concluded that the spiritual must be the cornerstone of health maintenance, and that to balance the physical and mental aspects of our lives we must tackle challenging activities while seeking love and friendship.

With these ideas he reflects Cayce's words on preparing for old age. When a correspondent asked, "How can I best prepare for old age?" Cayce answered in reading 3420–1, "By preparing for the present. Let age only ripen thee. For one is ever just as young as the heart and the purpose. Keep sweet. Keep friendly. Keep loving, if ye would keep young."

Traditional Medicine Views Edgar Cayce

My review of Dr. Reilly's accomplishments and thoughts soundly reinforced Edgar Cayce's credibility. Most interesting to me was how Reilly combined spiritual and mental growth with the importance of physical therapy as a supplement to medical practice. But what, I found myself asking, about opinions on the more "orthodox" side of the medical fence? What support if any would I find for Edgar Cayce's words among traditional doctors?

Randall A. Langston, M.D., is one of a growing number of physicians who have come to respect Cayce's unusual approach to health. In an afterword he wrote for Reba Ann Karp's classic volume *The Edgar Cayce Encyclopedia of Healing*, this traditionally trained and scientifically minded doctor tells how struck he was by the "rare interface between the metaphysical and scientific worlds." What impressed him most when he studied the history of Cayce's medical readings was how palpably ahead of their time they were. The consensus of the doctors who observed and evaluated Cayce's work at the time was characterized by Langston as: "Keep on doing what you're doing; someday we'll catch up."

One powerful example cited by Dr. Langston is Cayce's work on Alzheimer's disease, a degenerative disease of the central nervous system that is just beginning to be researched and understood today.

One of Cayce's recommendations for this still-mystifying disorder was to avoid cooking with aluminum utensils. At the time, it was hard to take such a suggestion

seriously. But many of Cayce's offbeat suggestions were
dismissed back then; the reasons they proved fruitful only
came to light later.

In this case, it was not until 1980 that reputable
scientific studies began pointing to aluminum as a factor
in brain cell damage. Then came the discovery of high
levels of aluminum in the brain cells of patients suffering
Alzheimer's disease. A lot more research still remains to
be done into this devastating illness, but there is no
avoiding the fact that Cayce's recommendation came at a
time when nothing in the traditional medical literature
linked aluminum with brain dysfunction.

Two physicians spearheading the drive to blend Edgar
Cayce's frequently exotic techniques with modern medical practice are the husband-and-wife team of William
and Gladys McGarey, both veteran M.D.'s of high standing. They were so impressed with Cayce's medical prowess that, as medical directors of the Edgar Cayce Foundation, they established the full-time A.R.E. clinic in
Phoenix, Arizona. From their clinic they coordinate a
growing group of physicians nationwide who supplement
their conventional practice with Cayce's specific recommendations and his spiritual teachings.

Dr. William McGarey was particularly impressed with
the results he obtained applying Cayce methods to the
insidious skin disease scleroderma. Though the illness is
not often seen by the average physician, it's effects are so
devastating that Dr. McGarey decided to issue a special
workbook on it so he could share what he learned with
his medical colleagues.

Scleroderma, a progressive illness that was looked on

as incurable, not only involves the surface skin but creates major systemic disorders of the heart, lungs, liver, and lymph system, leading eventually to death. As the disease progresses, the patient's skin can develop a stonelike hardness that draws the face into a mask. At this point the skin might actually chip like marble, with the skin becoming hardened more rapidly than it can be rebuilt. Meanwhile, the victim becomes immobilized as the sweat glands fail and the heart, lungs, and intestinal tract lose their functions, as do the thyroid, adrenals, and the liver.

When Cayce first turned his clairvoyant attention to the disease, he not only pinpointed a glandular malfunction as a basic cause, but he sensed the presence of a tubercle bacillus developed out of the deteriorated internal organs and lymph flow. Both conditions were later confirmed in the laboratory.

Dr. McGarey put Cayce's insights to use in several cases, the most critical being that of a twenty-eight-year-old woman for whom modern treatments had proved totally unsuccessful. When the Cayce regimen was used, the elements seemed oddly old-fashioned—but they were helpful.

For another patient, Dr. McGarey recommended several Cayce devices not generally taught in medical schools. He eventually wrote about them in a research bulletin distributed to his colleagues. Included was the consistent use of what is called a castor oil pack.

Castor Oil Packs

Of all of Cayce's devices for health and healing, one of the most ubiquitously recommended is the castor oil pack. In its method of operation it was a forerunner of the modern transdermal adhesive patch, used today to infuse doses of nitroglycerine through the skin of angina patients without placing stress on the internal organs. In a way, castor oil stands as a symbol of the Cayce mystery: not generally recognized in orthodox medical practice, it has been found to be unusually effective by the McGareys in their practice at the Phoenix clinic, even though they have not completely unraveled how it works.

Familiar to us from its old-time use as a laxative, castor oil is derived from a plant known as the *palma Christi,* translated as "palm of Christ," the name given it during the Middle Ages. To apply it (most often to the abdomen, but sometimes elsewhere in the treatment of injuries or lesions), three or four thicknesses of wool flannel are soaked in the warmed oil, then covered with a heating pad. This permits the curative effects to work their way through the skin and into the internal organs where they are needed. As with any medical therapy, I recommend the heating pad be used in consultation with a health-care professional. Care must of course be taken not to fall asleep with the heating pad turned on. After each use the skin is bathed with bicarbonate of soda.

The beneficial effects (despite their unknown mechanism) have been confirmed repeatedly in medical checkups. In his writing, Dr. McGarey said of this treatment, "Of all the therapies I have used in my practice of medicine, I have never found any that surpasses castor oil in its usefulness, its healing qualities, and its scope of therapeutic application." While he does consider faith in the treatment an important part of the picture, it's clear to him that the treatment in and of itself has therapeutic efficacy.

Visualization

Another important element in Dr. McGarey's treatment of scleroderma is visualization, a direct outgrowth of Cayce's conviction that "the spirit is the life, the mind is the builder, and the physical is the result."

In his research bulletin, McGarey didn't hesitate to fuse the "scientific" with the metaphysical, citing as his foundation the words of reading 326–1: "The body is spiritual in its aspects and in its reaction. . . . Vision self being aided by those applications [for example, the application of the castor oil pack]. Know what each application is for, seeing that DOING that within self. Keep the mind in that attitude as makes for CONTINUITY of forces manifesting through self—a continual flow, see?"

In addition to visualizing the good done by the treatment, Dr. McGarey stresses the value of meditation and prayer in invoking the healing forces that reside within us. "Keep the constructive forces in much of the prayer and meditation," Cayce recommended in reading 528–10.

"Raise that vibration within self that there are within self the healing forces. For all healing of every nature comes only from the One Source, the Giver of all good and perfect gifts."

What is unusual here is that in a medical bulletin, Dr. McGarey, a physician, is stressing to his colleagues the importance of the spiritual element in conventional medical practice. He is convinced that Cayce's message of visualization and prayer will help not only in scleroderma, but in the treatment of any disease. He also makes mention of a bit of Cayce advice that, while home-spun, should make sense to anyone, reflecting as it does the well-understood value of keeping a healthy attitude: "It will be necessary," says reading 528–12, "that the body NOT become OVER anxious or fretted. . . . Rather before or when this would occur, walk out in the open, take a circle around for five or ten minutes, and then commence all over again. But be constructive in the thought during those periods. And keep the mental attitudes!"

Psoriasis: Another Convincing Example

Dr. McGarey, through his extensive experience, has found that the Cayce recommendations discussed above have shown outstanding success where conventional medical measures have failed. The same can be said of the severe cases of psoriasis that were treated by Dr. John A. Pagano, a chiropractic physician who has, through his practice, developed a sturdy faith in Cayce's medical clairvoyance and put it to good use.

Well aware of the uncomfortable gap between traditional medicine and chiropractic, Dr. Pagano was pleased when several physicians of the conventional stripe urged him to write a paper on his successes treating this disorder that strikes some 150,000 Americans each year. His report demonstrates indisputably the effectiveness of Cayce's clairvoyant understanding about the disease.

The symptoms of psoriasis, itchy and sometimes painful skin lesions that in severe cases can result in total disability, have led traditional researchers to seek the cause in the skin surface. Utilizing Cayce's works, Dr. Pagano found that the lesions are a manifestation of the seepage of toxins through the thinning of the intestinal walls, resulting in toxification of the circulatory system and the lymphatics.

Following Cayce's detailed instructions, Dr. Pagano treated his patients with colonic irrigations, strict diet control, and specific herbal drinks. The latter included such exotic brews as American yellow saffron tea, slippery elm bark powder, chamomile, and mullein tea. These and other homey remedies were carried out according to a strict schedule, and were accompanied by chiropractic manipulations. The results shown in his paper create an affirmation of Cayce's clairvoyance that cannot be disputed.

Dr. Pagano launched his program on the basis of Cayce's belief expressed in reading 2455–2. When a woman asked Cayce simply, "Is there an absolute cure for psoriasis?" his reply was laconic but firm: "Most of this is found in diet. There is a cure. It requires patience, persistence, and right thinking also."

As to the "right thinking," Dr. Pagano concurs. In his paper he affirms Cayce's statement and draws a lesson for other physicians to heed: "It is an established fact not only in the readings but in modern science that the attitude of the patient—and the doctor—is as important as the therapy itself."

My own view, after reviewing the work of Cayce and those who have followed his teachings, is that anyone

facing a health problem should first take advantage of
the established accomplishments of modern medicine—
until and unless it becomes apparent that these techniques
have reached a blind alley. After all, the Cayce teachings
never discount the importance of using a trained physician. The teachings can, however, offer supplementary
options, especially when applied by physicians who recognize the value of unorthodox care when all else has
failed.

Holding On to Your Health: Nutrition

Having looked at some of Cayce's recommendations
for healing the sick, let's turn now to his advice for
guarding and maintaining good health in the normal
individual. The two areas he concentrates on—in addition to mental concentration and spiritual attunement, of
course—are nutrition and exercise. We'll look at nutrition
first.

Diet was so important to Cayce that he made reference to it when dealing with nearly every condition of
the human body. His reading 288–38 lay the groundwork for this constant attention to nutrition: "What we
think and what we eat—combined together—make what
we are physically and mentally." Reading 137–30 went
on to give instructions about the *way* we should eat:
"Never under strain, [or] when very tired, very ex-
cited, very mad, should the body take foods in the
system, see?"

Several other readings urge the sensible practice of
eating slowly, and not when we are overwrought. Today

these instructions seem routine, commonplace. But they were remarkable, even radical in their day, far ahead of their time.

Nearly all modern studies of nutrition reaffirm the homespun wisdom of Edgar Cayce. His recognition of pellagra, for instance, way back in the first decade of this century, in which he cited the cause as "too much hog and hominy," provoked a sustained medical attack on the disease. The vegetables he recommended in that case turned out to be ones rich in vitamin B complex, later found to be critical for the correction of this deficiency. Cayce also sounded an alarm about the nutritional short-comings of the American diet in general, a concern now reflected in the FDA regulations for food labeling, and in the modern-day warnings agaist the use of refined sugars, animal fats, and other enemies of good health.

On the subject of vitamins, Cayce was way ahead of his time, particularly in regard to the need for vitamin C, which has received so much attention these past few years. In reading 2072–9 he points out that the lack of this vitamin can bring about "bad eliminations from the incoordination of the excretory functioning of the alimentary canal, as well as the heart, liver and lungs." He adds a warning, however, about the overuse of supplementary vitamins, cautioning that a dependency on them might develop, or possibly even a toxic reaction. He would prefer that we concentrate on vitamin-rich foods, as many nutritionists recommend today.

There is space here to point out only the highlights of Cayce's elaborate dietary program, which is covered in exhaustive detail in the book *Edgar Cayce on Diet and*

Health, by Anne Reed, Carol Listrup, and Margaret Gammon. From my review of their book and other Cayce material, certain basic principles emerge.

While Cayce does not have much regard for red meats, for example, he does advocate the use of beef juice, which he feels produces salubrious effects on the salivary glands and on the gastric flow in general. He does approve of calves' liver, though, as well as fish, fowl, and lamb, as long as they are never fried.

Some of his ideas seem on the surface a little contradictory. Raw apples, for example, are regarded as beneficial as long as they are not taken with other foods, yet in another context he does include cooked apples in a group of foods he finds good for the health. These include unsulphured figs, prunes, small apricots, berries, dates, peaches, pears, raisins, and honey.

Other recommended fruits are grapefruit, oranges, limes, pineapple, and their juices, but herein lies an oddity: While Cayce feels cereals are good for the system, he warns they should not be taken at the same meal with citrus fruits. As he explains in reading 481-1, "This changes the acidity of the stomach to a detrimental condition; for citrus fruits will act as an eliminant when taken alone, but when taken with cereals it becomes as weight, rather than as an active force in the gastric forces of the stomach itself." A similar oddity is that he does not recommend cream or milk with coffee or tea; he claims this is hard on the digestion.

As to vegetables, Cayce feels it is helpful to mix those grown above the ground with those grown beneath it. Suggestions for mixing include asparagus, cauliflower, white cabbage, green peas, lettuce, spinach, sprouts, string beans, mushrooms, black olives, celery, onions, cooked turnips, sweet potatoes, rutabaga, parsnips, carrots, radishes, beets, and white potato skins. He finds potato skins particularly helpful, and in fact even suggests them as a poultice for various conditions.

Another basic regarding vegetables, brought out in reading 2602–1, is that we should have "at least one meal each day that includes a quantity of raw vegetables such as cabbage, lettuce, celery, carrots, onions, and the like. Tomatoes may be used in their season. . . . Have at least one leafy vegetable to every one of the pod vegetables taken."

In addition to dietary guidance meant to preserve good health, Cayce shaped special diets for people with specific disabilities. I must confess I have winced at some of these suggestions. For instance, he recommends eating raw Jerusalem artichokes for some cases of diabetes. I do happen to have a high sugar count; and someday I may get up the courage to eat a raw artichoke. So far I'm having enough trouble eating raw carrots, another recommendation I have made up my mind to try on the basis of documented results.

In the main, though, Cayce's dietary recommendations are sensible and easy to follow, as are his recommendations for regular exercise, which he feels should be part of our daily routine in our search for health and energy.

Exercise

With the importance Cayce places on stimulation of the body as a whole, naturally he advocates exercise as essential to good health. We will touch only briefly on the specifics of his exercise program, but there are certain principles that stand out and should be well heeded. One basic principle is his warning not to put stress on any single part of the body; instead we should exercise the full body so as to improve the system as a whole.

Exercise should be taken daily and regularly, by all means, and the morning is the perfect time to start. Cayce had great respect for the ordinary house cat as the ideal model for stretching and yawning upon waking. He said we could do no better than to emulate the way this animal slowly and gently puts its muscles into action. Not only should we begin our day with that picture in mind, but we should repeat the routine several times during the day as a break in our generally sedentary lives. This is a routine we can follow even while sitting in an office chair.

At the beginning of the day we should also carry out a few minutes of upright exercise, concentrating on those that involve the upper part of the body and the arms. One technique Cayce favors is bending backwards with the arms over the head; another is pivoting the upper torso with arms extended to the sides, swinging the body back and forth in the process.

Another favorite of Cayce's is the neck roll; he particularly recommends this in preparation for meditation. This exercise should be done sitting in an upright position and, as with most exercises, should be done slowly and gently. First the head is gently dropped forward to the chest three times. Then it is bent back—with reasonable force only—three times. Next the head is tilted to the right so that the ear almost touches the shoulder, also for three times, and finally the same process is repeated to the left. This simple exercise may be repeated several times during the day.

At night Cayce favors exercise done from a prone position, such as raising the legs and circling them, as well as bringing the head up to touch each knee several times.

Cayce lived long before our worldwide craze for jogging, but he does mention running—or simply running in place—as one option for vigorous exercise, if done with care. (As with any vigorous exercise program, you should check with your doctor for contraindications.) But by far the best exercise according to Cayce is walking in the open air for an optimum time of half an hour each day—a logical recommendation considering his emphasis on total body stimulation for systemwide good health.

Health: A Perfect Balance

Edgar Cayce's specific recommendations for preserving health through diet and exercise, as well as for restoring it once it has deteriorated, are clearly a direct outgrowth of his view that "the spirit is the life, the mind is the builder, and the physical is the result." Dr. William McGarey, writing about Cayce's holistic approach, agrees; we must recognize that body, mind, and spirit are all interconnected—in a sense are all one—and that we therefore can use "mental means and spiritual aids in reversing the pathological process." McGarey also stresses Cayce's concept that "all parts of the body must work together for the good of the whole and no part can function independently of the rest.''

McGarey's words remind me of a dramatic incident I witnessed that has haunted my memory for years. I was producing a documentary film for NBC-TV on microsurgery research at George Washington University Medical School. Using instruments fine enough to remove the nucleus from a cell, these researchers were actually tearing human cells apart as we watched through a powerful microscope.

The lens was focused on a carpet of healthy cells that seemed comfortably at rest. Suddenly, a single cell removed itself from the carpet and began to spin. Spinning furiously and apparently without purpose, it moved away from the carpet of fellow cells, dashing about like a water bug. I asked the researcher what was going to happen to it. ''Once it leaves the carpet it will die,'' he said.

I continued to watch through the eyepiece as the cell spun fruitlessly for a while; finally it stopped, floating like an island cut off from the mainland. The cell, after an intoxicating time on its own, was dead.

That little incident has hung in my mind for a long time. It serves as an allegory, making the point that a living unit must remain one with its source, whether it is a person trying to break away from society, or an organ rebelling against the work it must do within the human body.

Dr. McGarey makes that very point when he writes, ''Health . . . involves coordinating the functions of all the organs and systems of the human body.'' He goes on to say that health is not achieved simply by taking antibiotics or submitting to an operation, for health, as he defines it, is "a state of perfect balance," and healing is "that which brings that kind of balance again."

Nor, according to McGarey, is this balance merely a physical one. Like all of life's processes, it is a reflection of a spiritual reality, as expressed in Cayce's reading 2696–1, which McGarey cites:

"For all healing comes from the one source. And whether there is the application of foods, exercise, medicine, or even the knife—it is to bring the consciousness of the forces within the body that aid in reproducing themselves—the awareness of Creative, or God, Forces."

QUESTION 5

How Can I Work and Love at My Highest Capacities?

A couple of decades ago I had lunch with one of Sigmund Freud's closest associates, Theodor Reik, at the Algonquin Hotel in New York. At the time I was writing a column on books and publishers for the *Saturday Review,* and he had just published a new book. I found Dr. Reik a fascinating subject to interview: a distinguished gentleman of the old school, witty and perceptive.

By then I had read enough books about psychoanalysis to be quite confused by the mass of Freudian obscurities, so I thought I'd ask Dr. Reik to boil down the practice to its absolute essence. I assumed there must be one compressed target that the analyst aims toward with every patient. It was probably unfair to ask Dr. Reik to reduce Freud's enormous volumes to a single sentence, but he graciously accepted the challenge.

"Yes," he said, "I can acommodate you on that question. We have one single purpose at the end of all our psychoanalytic therapy, and this is to have all patients reach a point where they can work and love at their highest capacity."

Dr. Reik then elaborated, saying that this target applies not only to the neurotic and the psychotic, but to the person with no serious emotional problems as well. "If people can work and love at their highest capacity," he explained, "they are manifestly free of neurosis or psychosis." Then he added—almost casually—that work and love are tightly bound together and firmly interwoven.

Edgar Cayce may not have been a psychoanalyst, but his psychic readings certainly point to the same conclusion about love and work, if for different—in Cayce's case spiritual—reasons. In fact, Cayce's understanding of the human mind might be said to be closer to the collective unconscious of psychologist Carl Jung than to the theories of Freud or Reik: Jung's collective unconscious posits a psychical inheritance of racial experience—a pool of memory that resides in every member of the race; Cayce believed everyone's unconscious is interlocked, which is what permitted him to leap across time and space to make his exacting medical diagnoses and to tune in to the Universal Forces for rare cosmic insights.

For Cayce, love is spiritual because—to put it simply, as he did over and over—God is love. In fact, what he says is that God is love and that love is God; and since he also has said that God is all there is, we might assume he also means that love is all there is.

In the book *A Search for God*, compiled by the original A.R.E. study group in Virginia Beach, the text says, "Love is God. The whole law is fulfilled in these three words. Mankind is urged to observe and to cultivate this attribute for it is through love that physical life is perfected and the continuity of life realized. Life is the Creative Force in action and is the expression of love.'' With the Creative Force being infinite and omnipresent, that means the supply of love is unlimited and its abundance is always available.

No wonder, then, that both Reik and Cayce tell us that love and work are inseparable.

Nonetheless, I intend to separate them—temporarily, for the purposes of answering the central question of this chapter: ''How can I work and love at my highest capacities?'' As we'll see when we discuss work later in the chapter, this separation is really impossible: it's love, says Cayce, that forms the bedrock of good work; and certainly our functioning in the workplace is affected by the relationships we maintain there. But when people say they wish to improve the quality of ''love'' in their life, they often are speaking of their personal relationships— their friendships, family structures, sex, and romance. And so I intend to look first at what Cayce says about enhancing those relationships, and then to explore the role of love in the workplace.

To begin, let's look at the spiritual dimensions of love.

What Is Love?

The Cayce readings, like so many other spiritual teachings, tell us not only that God is love, but that all of creation is an expression of the spirit of God. This is emphasized over and over as Cayce refers to the Divinity as the Creative Force. In reading 281–24 he asks the rhetorical question, "When matter comes into being, what has taken place?" then answers it this way: "The Spirit ye worship as God has *moved* in space and in time to make for that which gives its expression; perhaps as wheat, as corn, as flesh. . . ." Our own beings are the result of the action of His spirit. We bear His imprint upon our souls—the imprint of divine love. Realizing this is the key to effectiveness in work, in love, or in any other area of life.

One attribute of this divine spirit that resides at the center of our beings is its impulse to manifest itself, to make itself felt through our actions. This impulse is like the "divine itch" we discussed in Question 2 that impels us toward our true purpose in life, guided by our spiritual ideal. It is all part and parcel of recognizing and joining with the Creative Force.

So it is with love, according to Cayce. When our actions express the love of God, we are acting in accord with the Creative Force that sustains the whole universe. We are then able to draw upon its power in all our actions.

But humans are free-willed beings. We can choose to reflect God's love in our actions, or we can choose to pursue selfish goals, unloving ones that are not compatible with the Creative Force that gives us life. In so doing, Cayce warns, we are working at cross-purposes with our innermost selves, and as a result our efforts will eventually come to nothing.

Cayce acknowledged our free will, and the options available for us to choose among, in reading 352–1. "There are two ways lying before the entity," he said.

"These may be chosen *best* by self; for the gift of the Creative influence is . . . the abilities to make self, through the application of will, one with the constructive influences or to turn same to self's own indulgencies."

Having acknowledged free will, Cayce then made clear the possible consequences of its exercise: "And those that seek to know self"—meaning those who seek attunement with the Creative Force within them—"may find . . . joy, peace, happiness, even though the way be hard."

But "those that look for self-indulgencies, . . . without being tempered with the true love as of the Father . . . , *these* find those things that make for hardships, strifes, turmoils, even though there are—from the *material* standpoint—abundances"

To avoid working against ourselves in this way, no matter what the endeavor, the first step is to know ourselves. To a questioner who asked whether a particular field he was considering would be "the most successful and remunerative," Cayce answered in reading 969–1, "Most successful and most remunerative, provided *first* that self is located. What are you trying to do? Something for [yourself], to be exalted before men? Or something for the love that [you have] for [your] fellow man . . . ?"

People seeking guidance from the readings on how to find fulfillment in their careers as well as in their relationships with others were repeatedly advised to define very clearly just what they worshiped as God. What did they want to serve—divine love, or self-interest? Serving God, Cayce told them all, is the way to inner peace, joy, and contentment. Working for self-indulgence might bring apparent success for a time, but in the long run setting the purposes of the conscious mind against those of the spirit of God within us naturally and inevitably produces turmoil.

First, Love God

Almost a prerequisite for serving God is, of course, loving Him. That's why one commandment is scattered throughout the readings: "Thou shalt love the Lord thy God with all thy heart, all thy mind, all thy strength . . . and thy neighbor as thyself."

For Cayce, this is the most important foundation of life for all of us, and nothing should supersede this. I must confess that loving God—whether an abstract God or an anthropomorphic one—is extremely difficult for me to visualize and hence to put into practice, though I can see what a desirable state of mind that would be. I hope someday to achieve it, simply on the recommendation of wiser heads than mine who have embraced the idea wholeheartedly.

But I have trouble doing this—at least completely. Even setting this as a conscious ideal, I feel like the blind man in a dark room looking for a black cat that doesn't exist. After tracking Cayce's ideas through his readings, though, a few shafts of light have pierced the dark room, so maybe I'm making a little headway. Cayce's general line of thought seems to imply that if we cannot sense God palpably, we can at least be aware of His manifestations. That's not too hard to do sitting on a New England mountainside at the height of the autumn foliage. Nor is it all that difficult when I look on the face of my sleeping five-year-old son. Even when he breaks into a mischievous romp, that manifestation is still obviously there.

So I guess I *am* finding that there are ways to follow Cayce's urging to put the love of God before everything else. One way to practice it is to follow the Biblical commandment: when we love our neighbor as ourselves, we are indirectly expressing our love for God, since God is all there is.

Of course, love is pretty hard to trap in a measuring cup, and even harder to analyze. Dr. Rollo May, the astute psychiatrist and author of the brilliant book *Love and Will*, points out that there are four kinds of love in the Western tradition: the sex/lust drive, or libido; the drive to procreate, called eros; the brotherly, friendship kind of love, or philia; and the benevolent concern for the welfare of others, or agape, which expresses the love of God for man.

While Cayce certainly doesn't eschew libido or eros—as we'll see later, he frequently addressed these forms of love in his readings—as might be expected he places the greatest weight on agape and philia, with his emphasis on manifesting the love *of* God through brotherly love, and expressing love *for* God by serving the welfare of others.

Whatever happens in the external world, Dr. May writes, "human love and grief, pity and compassion are what matter." He reinforces this by saying, "We have defined agape as esteem for the other, the concern for the other's welfare beyond any gain that one can get out of it; disinterested love, typically, the love of God for man." Cayce, it seems to me, would not have said this any differently.

Love Is Giving

What Cayce did say, in fact, is that there is a "law of love," which he defines in reading 3744–4 with a single word: giving. His basic advice is contained in reading 341–44, where he says, "For if ye would have love, give. If ye would have life, give."

In other words, love is giving. In reading 3744–4 he tells us that if we look about us we will see "upon the physical or earth or material plane the manifestations of that law." But he also warns us that "the gift, the giving, with hope of reward or pay is direct opposition of the law of love." To truly love as God loves, we must give without any desire for reward. As soon as our "loving" is accompanied by the hope of repayments, as soon as we attach any strings at all to what we do for others, we are no longer giving. We are no longer manifesting divine love, and we have cut ourselves off from the full power of the Creative Force. The end result is that we will have limited our capacity to love and work effectively.

So how *do* we go about creating the most fully loving relationships we can have with others? The first step is an internal one. The readings phrase it as being "approved" by God and our ideal. This involves adopting the best, most nearly divine motivation we can conceive of. This is our ideal on the spiritual level, which Cayce describes in reading 256–2, as, "something to look up to, or to attempt to *attain* to." We can then choose attitudes, patterns of thought, and physical actions that conform to our ideal.

In reading 3744–4, Cayce tells us to remember that

"there is no greater than the injunction, 'God so loved His Creation, or the World, as to Give His Only Begotten Son, for their redemption.' " Now, Cayce is not necessarily telling us to sacrifice our own children, but he is holding up a most sublime example of giving with no thought but for the betterment of someone else. If we can make our actions conform to our ideal in all our relationships, we will then be doing our best to manifest divine love toward others—in other words, to love at our highest capacity.

One source to turn to for guidance and stability as we study to know our ideal, one that's always handy because it resides within us, is the Christ consciousness. The love that emanated from Jesus, Cayce tells us, can serve to light the way. Cayce's implication is that when Jesus said, "I am the Way, the truth, and the life," He was suggesting that we ourselves could be "the Way," that we all have the capacity to do all that He did. It's all a matter of reaching for that ideal.

Whatever our beliefs about Jesus, there's plenty of evidence that we are capable of living out the biblical concept "Greater love hath no man than that he lay down his life for his friend." My reading of history shows me so many examples of this—from every culture and every time—that I believe it must be an almost instinctual action that reflects love expressed at our highest capacity.

Not everyone's life presents the chance for such dramatic self-sacrifice, of course. Nor is self-sacrifice the sole criterion for whether we are truly loving. But if we are guided by our ideal, Cayce says, then we will know that love founded in the spirit of God within does not depend on our being rewarded, which means it does not depend on the other person's reactions for its strength.

"For what is the gain if ye love those ONLY that love thee?" Cayce asks in reading 987–4. To express this type of love we will keep on giving even if our love is not reciprocated. We will give even if we are hurt in return. In fact, the hurt that we feel as human beings serves as a sign that an effort in the right direction is being made. We should therefore take no notice of injuries done us, and instead apply the Golden Rule even to those we are having difficulty with. "To bring hope, to bring cheer, to bring joy, yea to bring a smile again to those whose face and heart are bathed in tears and in woe is but making that divine love SHINE—SHINE—in thy own soul!" And since this ideal love is given with no thought of repayment, it comes straight from the heart, and complete sincerity and honesty are among its most natural characteristics.

This advice, of course, is highly idealized. Few of us can express this divinely pure love consistently. But we can *try*. The reason we must try, according to reading 1537–1, is that "hate *creates*, as does love—and brings turmoils and strifes." Like hate, loving patterns of thought and action build upon themselves. The more persistently we try to act in accord with this pattern of divine love, the closer we come to attaining it within ourselves. And so applying our best conception of divine love as often and as completely as we can, Cayce teaches, is the strongest move we can make in developing our ability to love at our highest capacity.

Love Is Not Ownership

What are some of the other characteristics of this divine kind of love?

Since it is shared without recompense, it is completely undemanding and unpossessive; it finds no fault in others. Cayce spells this out clearly in reading 1816–1, where he states, "And remember the new commandment, 'Love one another.' Not in a possessive manner. O that all would learn that LOVE is all-embracing, and NOT merely possession."

A kind of Catch-22 does seem inherent in any love that makes demands. Evidence spread across the historical and literary landscape of love and lovers show that the tighter one tries to rein in the object of one's love, the more likely one is to be the loser. Perhaps this is because by controlling and reshaping the person you love, you prevent him or her from being the very person you at first loved. This is a catch that can apply to friendship as easily as to romance.

Express Love through Service

Another quality of this unselfish love is, naturally, that it is expressed most fully in service to those around us. It offers hope to the discouraged, cheer to the despondent. And it is joyful: since it flows from the spirit of God within each of us, it is in the manifestation of that spirit that true happiness is experienced.

I once researched a story that drove home to me the joy that can be found in service to others.

Devastating tornadoes had ripped across miles of territory in Ohio and Pennsylvania. Several towns were flattened and nearly a hundred people killed. The destruction was incomprehensible. Because the area struck was not part of the so-called Tornado Alley of the Great Plains, the population was totally unprepared for such a display of nature's fury. As I interviewed survivors, at first I found nothing but agonizing despair and hopelessness.

But then something happened. A spirit of love and service came over the people. They rallied to help one another to such a degree that their despair was transformed into a new spirit of love and affection.

Mayor Helen Dubie of Wheatland, Pennsylvania, told me of an incident that to this day she considers the most moving experience of her life. She was touring an area of almost total destruction in her town. She hadn't slept in three days, and as she stumbled through the streets she felt crushed and helpless at the sight of such loss. Then a woman crawled out from the ruined cellar of her house, threw her arms around the mayor, and said, "Have you been hugged today?" At once Mayor Dubie was filled with the courage and strength to go on with the massive job of reconstruction.

Dozens of incidents emerged from this horrid tragedy that reflect genuine love expressed through service to others—including making the ultimate sacrifice. One man, seeing a tornado heading directly toward him and the two children with him, threw the children into a ditch and threw himself on top of them. The man was ripped away by the winds and thrown hundreds of yards to his death, but the children survived, recipients of his gift of unselfish love.

Reflecting a love of community for community were the actions of the Amish and Mennonites, who came from miles away to help rebuild the stricken towns. Leaving behind the work of their own farms, they brought their own tools with them and spent weeks moving up and down the demolished streets, clearing away rubble and helping to rebuild the houses of strangers they had never even seen before. One Mennonite leader explained to me that all he wanted to do was to "put the love of Christ into action."

Months after this day of killer tornadoes the people were settled again, imbued now with a rich feeling of love they had never known before—the inheritance of unselfish service to others.

Cayce's counsel, of course, does not have to await such dramatic circumstances as these. Service to others on a daily basis can also bring its rewards. As he told his questioner in reading 3659–1, we should apply "self... towards being a means of help to someone else. And let the joy of this alone bring its own reward in peace and harmony, and in a pleasing personality."

Love Is Joyful

Over and over Cayce uses the word "joy" in talking of the experience of love and service. It seems to be a natural product of applying ourselves in the service of others, and so becomes our automatic reward for that service.

More than just a reward, though, it can be a guiding principle. Cayce advises us repeatedly that our daily life should be pursued joyfully. Life is not to be "made long-faced, that no joy is to enter in!" he says in reading 480–20. "Rather be ye *joyous* in thy *living,* in thine association, in thy activities, ever. For joy and happiness *beget* joy and happiness; unless the import be of a *selfish* nature."

Humor, for me, is a form of joy by which we can express our true love and affection. Victor Borge once said, "A laugh is the shortest distance between two people," which tells me that a laugh can translate into love.

One way I have overcome my resistance to understanding the elusive love of God is by speculating that God must have a sense of humor, or we wouldn't have one ourselves. In fact, I think it's a great disservice that most theologians fail to point this out—which is why, I imagine, Cayce so often stressed joy and humor and cautioned against a downcast demeanor. Jesus Himself, the way I read Scripture, was not against bringing humor into his own teachings. I can't seem to read His words, "It is easier for a camel to go through the eye of a needle than for a rich man to enter into the kingdom of God," without picturing it as a hilarious—if instructive—cartoon.

Humor can also, I believe, play a strong role in healing, perhaps because of its connection with love. Edgar Cayce was a strong proponent of the part love plays in healing. In the A.R.E. book *Face to Face,* Herbert Puryear points out that spiritual healing *does* occur, even in cases considered incurable, because "when the spirit of life and light and love is quickened in one person, it may be projected by thought and prayer to quicken the spirit of life in another."

Norman Cousins, in his best-selling book *Anatomy of an Illness*, tells how humor—for him merely an expression of his unbounded love for the whole human race—brought about his own recovery from a disease he was told was incurable. He was so convinced that laughter could be a therapeutic agent that he designed his own program for recovery around it, following a daily regiment of Marx brothers' movies, *Candid Camera* episodes, and the like. He's still around years later to talk about his success.

Sexual Love

This divinely inspired love we are discussing can be expressed in all our relationships—in the family, among friends, or between sexual lovers. But to many people the most insistent facet of the question "How can I love at my highest capacity?" is really "How can I find the most fulfillment in my sex life?"

Our basic choice with regard to sex is the same as it is concerning the use of any of our other attributes: Whom will we serve—God, or self?

When asked by a questioner in reading 1173-11 by what standards our motives for marriage should be measured, Cayce gave an answer addressing all sexual relationships: "There should be sought as to whether the relationships . . . are for a united, cooperative service to a living God and of a spiritual prompting, or are they prompted by material desires?

"If they are prompted by . . . convenience," he advised, "or for only the beauty of the body . . . these must become palls one upon the other. . . . There must be the ANSWERING within each that their SPIRITUAL and MENTAL desires are ONE!'' In other words, we must ask ourselves whether we will use sex for self-gratification only, or to create spiritual blessings in the lives of others.

As free-willed beings, either path is open to us. But as you might guess, the attitude of the readings toward sex is consistent with their perspective on all other phases of life. We can choose to use sex only to please ourselves—and perhaps we will be outwardly successful in this pursuit for a time. But the way to achieve a true and lasting contentment is to use sex to express the beauty and love of the Creative Forces.

I'm reminded of a friend of mine, a divorced man who seemed able to have his way with almost any woman he wanted to pursue. I asked him how he was enjoying this Don Juan state of affairs, and he surprised me by answering, ''I've finally come to a conclusion: There's nothing more monotonous than variety.'' I can imagine Cayce nodding his head in agreement, and perhaps commenting, as he did in reading 1479–1, that the purpose of sexual love should be ''not just the aggrandizement of a material or earthly or body passion,'' that what was missing was the spiritual dimension.

Depending on the individual, using sex to express the love of the Creative Forces might mean using it only for procreation. But for someone else it might mean engaging in sexual activity for the purpose of bringing joy into the life of another person. That both of these are options is made clear in reading 826–6, where Cayce was asked whether ''continence'' should prevail except for the production of offspring.

"For some, yes," he answered; "in other cases it would be *very* bad on the part of each, while in others it would be bad on one or the other, see?"

What matters is carrying out our soul's spiritual purposes, however that is put into practice: "There should be, then, rather the educating as to the *purposes,* and *how* . . . the gratifying of emotions may be centralized in creating—in the lives of others about the body in all its various phases—spiritual blessings."

This can even apply to sex outside of marriage, as Cayce made clear further on in the same reading, provided it "is a matter of principle within the individual." It's here that Cayce said quite explicitly that "it is as natural for there to be sexual relations . . . as it is for the flowers to bloom in the spring, or for the snows to come in the winter." The legitimizing factor is whether it is consistent with the individual's principles and whether it is done as an expression of his or her ideal.

Just as legitimate an option is to remain celibate and use the energy of the sex drive to fuel one's loving, creative efforts in a completely different area of life, but only if that is the individual's choice. Choice—and staying true to that choice—is the key here, as Cayce said in the reading: "When a man or woman has chosen (for it must be choice . . .) to not be in such relationships, then be true to the choice. . . . For that which one would pretend to be and isn't is indeed sin!" I have to believe that Cayce is talking here about sexual hypocrisy, something we've become more familiar with these days than we would like.

Cayce's bottom line then, as explained in reading 5747-3, is that the biological sex drive should be purified in service to God, in the expressions of love, "which are: gentleness, kindness, brotherly love, long-suffering," and that this be done in whatever way best fits the individual's purpose in life.

The Role of Love in the Workplace

For some people, applying Edgar Cayce's prescription for effective living to the workplace might be harder than applying it to their personal relationships. They might be willing to concede that expressing love is important in relating to others—that's obvious—but what in the world does it have to do with making a living?

A central assumption of the Cayce readings is that God is One, and therefore He is God of every phase of our lives—religious, psychic, mental, emotional, physical, and financial. Cayce made this point in reading 4405–1, when he acknowledged that "oft it is considered by individuals that the spiritual life and mental life are things apart. They *must* be one," he corrected, "they *are* one, even though individuals attempt to separate." In fact, "the *spirit* is the life, the motive force . . . behind all life itself."

Because God's spirit has dominion over all, in Cayce's view, there is no true separation between the spiritual and, say, the financial; the spiritual, after all, is properly a component of everything we do. As a result, the principle of divine love that lies behind our best way of relating to others is just as applicable in our work lives.

As spiritual as the Cayce material on working effectively is, though, it is also extremely practical. Many people familiar with Cayce's work know that readings for physical health were the most common type of readings he gave. But few people realize that business was the readings' second most common topic.

Back to the Foundation

The foundation of Cayce's advice on working at our highest capacities probably sounds familiar by now: God, or the Creative Force, is love; when we work in harmony with divine love we are able to draw upon His infinite power; when our efforts are selfish, unloving, we close ourselves off to that power. This reasoning lay at the heart of the advice Cayce gave to a questioner who was considering changing his life's work. In reading 853–2 Cayce suggested the man ask himself: "Does the life's [current] work lead to those conditions that make for antagonisms with [God's] will, as understood by self?" If so, then the advice was to make the change to daily labor that would be more in accord with what the man had "set as an ideal service to Him." But if "that in which the body is [currently] engaged [gives an] opportunity for service to thy fellow man, . . . then use that as a way . . . of exemplifying *His* will"—at least for now. Don't give up this method of giving service until all its opportunities have been explored.

Added to this is the assurance that if we are working for the glory of God rather than self, all our financial needs will be met. Cayce made that promise quite directly in reading 877–2: "When the body sets itself in those capacities . . . wherein the body may serve, he will be . . . insuring himself respecting his future income, his future material success, his future material and social acitivities.''

Cayce cited biblical passages as illustrative of this principle: the lilies of the field, who toil not, neither do they spin; the birds of the air, who sow not but are fed by God. But Cayce also anticipated skepticism on this point, as he said in reading 1472–6: "Yea, ye call this impractical— for ye are in a practical and a commercial and a business world.'' Nonetheless, he assured his questioner, ''Yes, it will come to thee if ye apply thyself,'' suggesting he ask himself the following questions to understand the mechanism: "Who IS the silver and the gold? Who IS the power, the might, the light, the hope? Who is the giver of these?'' God, Cayce taught, as the Lord of all creation, is Lord of the material wealth of the universe and will put it in your service if you are working in His.

Where to Start

The first step in working at our highest capacities is to choose the field in which to engage. And the first step in doing that is to become clear in our mind what we are working for. According to the readings, we will find the greatest fulfillment if we choose a career in which we are most able to express our spiritual ideal. It is possible, of course, to work only for self-aggrandizement and to achieve material success in this way. But such work is contrary to the deepest life purpose of the soul, and it will eventually result in inner turmoil as our actions run counter to the will of the Creative Force that resides inescapably within us.

Once our direction has been set, the next step is to prepare ourselves. This may involve getting whatever formal training we need. It may involve developing our abilities by working in an area related to the one we have chosen for our major contribution. Or it may involve internally rededicating ourselves to the purpose for which we will be working. In reading 877–2, Cayce expressed the need for such work this way: "First make the preparation from within.... Dedicate self; making those necessary activities for insuring self... that there needs to be little fear *ever* to enter [the chosen line of work]. For he that does so doubting already *invites* that which would bring corruption, dissension. But he that does so in the assurance that the promises are true, the promises are thine *own,* is insuring self and making secure."

Whatever field we choose, Cayce tells us, and whatever we must do to prepare ourselves, our preparation will make us more able and willing to achieving the purpose we have chosen to work for. Even in a reading (956–1) in which Cayce gave specific advice about the line of work his questioner was most suited to—vocational guidance— he still stressed the importance of preparation: both academic study and internal dedication. Asked when the questioner might expect to start such work, Cayce answered: "When preparations are made! That ye prepared yourself for, that ye become! As one prepares for the indwelling with the Creative Forces, then one may expect to enter into the joys of the Lord."

"If Only..."

An important point that Cayce made repeatedly is that we must always begin where we are. This seems self-evident, but an awful lot of us mark time in our jobs, thinking, "If only I were in such-and-such a situation, I'd really be able to move." Well, we're not in such-and-such a situation. We are where we are. It might not be the absolute best place for us, but if we must move, this is where we must move from. Today's opportunities can be used only under today's conditions. "If only" doesn't get the work done.

Closely related to this is the readings' frequent advice to "use that in hand." Wishing for different resources is no more effective than wishing to be in a different situation. This is exactly what Cayce told a questioner who wondered whether the New Year would bring better opportunities. "These are part of self's own development," he said in reading 1472–9, "and must rise within by taking advantage of those opportunities which are offered from day to day. As has so oft been indicated, . . . it is as we use that in hand that the greater opportunities are given." Use what is yours to use today—your motivation, knowledge, experience, ability, and material equipment. If your purpose is compatible with the Creative Force, Cayce promises, then God will make sure that today's resources are sufficient for today's tasks, and what you need tomorrow will come.

Just Do It!

Perhaps the tersest advice the readings ever gave to someone asking how to be successful was, "Just do it!" Once we've done what we can to make ourselves willing and capable of achieving our purpose, we should begin to apply ourselves in "concentrative effort" toward this goal. Even if we can't see all the steps that may be necessary, we have the assurance that, as we do what we know how to do, the next step will be shown to us.

It's important to understand, though, just what's meant by concentrative effort. "Not to dig in and worry, and fret," Cayce explained in reading 5603-3, "and to worry other people and to worry self as to whether it's getting along or not! Just *doing* it! and know that one applying self in any direction receives that which [one gives] *out*!"

Many of us like to procrastinate, hoping maybe if we delay we will be better equipped to tackle the job later. There's a poem by Goethe that has done wonders for me in this regard:

Are ye in earnest?
Seize this very minute.
What you can do, or dream you can—begin it.
Boldness has genius, power and magic in it.
Only engage, and then the mind grows heated;
Begin and then the work will be completed.

I'm sure I'm not taking liberties in saying Cayce would agree with Goethe a hundred percent. I know I do. I can't count the number of times I've sat at a typewriter convinced I was not ready to start writing. With this thought of Goethe's in mind, and with Cayce's advice to deal with what I have immediately at hand, I've found that the simple act of beginning to type can bring unexpected power with it. The mind actually does become heated; the action dredges up ideas from the unconscious, where they've been waiting to be called into service. This advice, I believe, applies to any activity that might be thought of as work, whether it's making important decisions or simply writing a letter you've been postponing far too long.

Once you begin, of course, you have to stick with it, which is why perseverance is another quality highly recommended in the readings. One woman was told that, for her, the greatest service to God and her fellow man could be achieved through a career in writing. She was warned, though, that success might be a long time in coming and that she should be prepared to "Write— write—write! Though ye may tear up for a year, or for more than a year, everything ye write...," Cayce told her in reading 1567–2, "ye will find the abilities to bring into the experience and minds of others the joys that are not even comprehended in the present!" In other words, this was the field in which her greatest contribution to mankind could be made, and it should be persevered in until the effort finally bore fruit.

To Love Is to Give

"Love is the giving out of that within self," said Cayce in reading 262–44. As we go about striving for the goal we have chosen to work toward, one thing we must do if we want our efforts to be attuned to the Creative

Force of love is to *give*. We receive what we give out in life, Cayce teaches, and so if we want to attain more than run-of-the-mill fulfillment from our work, we must be willing to give more than run-of-the-mill service each day.

Reading 361–9 speaks of it this way: "For he that is the greatest servant is the lord of the many, and he that seeks in the life's service and the life's activity to give not just a day's labor but more, not just making the grade but willing and active in making MORE!"

Luckily, we have models we can follow for this: Jesus as He acted in the world, and the Christ consciousness that resides within us. "This is as He lived," Cayce reminds us, "and only asks that each follow in His way." We should not, however, become sanctimonious just because we are doing what we ought. "If thy activity in living thy ideal makes thee as one aloof," Cayce cautions, "something then is wrong. If it makes thee better as a social companion, this is the right." And really, when you think about it, if this truly is love we are practicing, how can it possibly make us aloof?

A Word about Our "Enemies"

"Do I have any enemies of whom I must be careful?" Cayce was asked in reading 2953–1. "Yes," was the quick reply, "the greatest enemy is self, as it is with everyone else. . . . Enemies are only those who are selfish in themselves."

In our work, as in every other aspect of our lives, we must treat those about us lovingly—which means we must be on the lookout for envy, anger, and resentment within us and replace them with more loving responses. And of course we must not cater to greed.

Over the short term, it may seem that a certain amount of advancement and material well-being can be won by taking unfair advantage of those we do business with. But in the long run, the readings tell us, only by working in concert with the Creative Force can we prosper and find fulfillment.

In counseling someone troubled by envy toward a business associate who was receiving undeserved favor and advancement, Cayce pointed out that though this person might be enjoying material prosperity, he was also suffering inner turmoil and was definitely not to be envied. Speaking broadly in reading 531–3 Cayce reminded his questioner, "There come periods in thine experience when doubts arise . . . , and thou sees about thee those that disregard law, order, or even the rights of their fellow man—yet from the material angle they APPEAR to succeed in gaining more of this world's goods. And they are apparently entrusted with the activities . . . that will have to do with the lives . . . of many souls. Then thou, in thy ignorance, proclaim: 'What is the use of trying to be good?' . . . But hast thou looked into their hearts and seen the trouble and doubt there? Hast thou looked into their lives . . . and seen the fear, the doubt, the shame even often that crouches there?" In one tidy package Cayce gave his questioner reason to be on guard against two internal enemies: envy and greed.

Hostility too is something to be avoided, as much in the workplace as in our personal lives. In reading 603–2 Cayce tells us to rise above anger and resentments against our associates that may arise out of personal conflicts. This inquirer had a particular associate who was causing him great distress. He asked Cayce what he could do about it.

Here Cayce came up with an interesting suggestion: an attitude of "loving indifference." The recommendation was, "Where there may be aid given, give it. But busy thyself rather in other fields of activity, letting the indifference be as an act of service in other directions."

For still another case, reading 262–47, Cayce expanded on the development of a loving condition by stating, "Let the love that was manifested in forgiveness be in thee, that there be no envy, no strife, no knowledge of other than good works through the activities of self."

To do this, Cayce suggests in reading 2629–1, we should practice the tool of tolerance. "The application of love as related to tolerance is the greater virtue," Cayce explained. "Thus in thy dealings with others, magnify their virtues, minimize their faults. For, even as the Lord condemned no one, even as He forgave, so would you forgive."

Does all this self-improvement, all this guarding against internal enemies, seem a pretty tall order to fill? Are you already set to criticize yourself for failing to accomplish it it overnight? Cayce has a word of reassurance about that too: impatience, after all, with yourself as well as with others, is just another of those internal enemies of loving expression.

"Do not become overanxious because [these qualities] have prevented a greater culmination of the abilities," Cayce said in reading 270–34. "Do not become impatient. Learn patience with self as well as with others, for in patience ye become aware of your soul."

Now, Cayce did not have to be clairvoyant to point out the importance of patience. But because those who wrote to Cayce for guidance had profound respect for his authority, the answer, simple as it is, struck home with enough impact to make a difference in their lives. In reviewing his words, I too have found myself wondering about my own capacity for patience. I'm afraid I would rate about a minus 100 on the Patience Scale. But just thinking this over has actually helped me work for increased patience, so I guess I have to admit the advice worked.

The central point of the Edgar Cayce readings about working at our highest capacities is that the results of our labor are not to be measured in terms of material security. The vital consideration is how well we have expressed the Creative Force of love through our work. When we align ourselves with the love of God, we can be sure that we will attain the inner fulfillment that comes from working in harmony with His will, which lives at the heart of our being.

Cayce as much as promises this fulfillment, and in fact tells us it is the proof that we are doing well, when he reminds us in reading 531-3, "When thou speakest kindly and gently to thine associates, to thine own house, to thine own neighbors, dost thou not find that thy heart and soul sings for joy because of that thou hast made in the experience of those to whom thou hast spoken—even though there arise turmoils in the secular things of life?

"So is life. So is thine soul growing to fruition. . . ."

Summarizing, Cayce encourages us, "Be not weary in

well-doing. He that endureth unto the end will wear the crown of joy, of life, of a contented soul.''

This approach is not only spiritual; it is extremely down-to-earth. To work at our highest capacities we must be willing to get our hands dirty. We must be willing to roll up our sleeves and sweat. But before we start, we should have a very clear idea just Who it is we will be sweating for.

QUESTION 6

How Can I Get Rid of Frustrations, Hostility, and Negative Attitudes?

Sometimes I think I should install a kind of taxi meter on my desk so I could flip down the flag and charge myself for all the time I waste with negative thinking. A device like that would cost me a pretty penny, particularly for the time spent dwelling on hostile thoughts, a pastime that ends only in frustration because nothing ever comes of it. (Maybe that's a good thing; if anything did come of my hostility, it would probably be an assault-and-battery charge before the judge.)

I would bet all of us waste time now and then reveling in the fantasy of someone dangling from a noose. Maybe that "enemy" did something outrageous to provoke our anger; then again, maybe we've only been projecting. Either way, the one thing that seems clear is that, as we dwell on negative feelings, we ourselves are the ones being hurt. At best we fritter away time and energy that would be better put to creative pursuits. Worse, we may even be harming our health. Anger, Cayce points out, can actually have an impact on the natural functions of the body, disturbing our circulation, glandular, and digestive systems. We mislead ourselves, he says in one reading, if we think that we can have a motivation of resentment in what he calls our "mental bodies" and not feel its impact on our physical bodies. Certainly it's bad for blood pressure and can cause ulcers.

Worst of all, anger and resentments can propel us to act contrary to the better influences of our lives, disastrously reducing our chances for real spiritual attunement and growth.

Recognizing the damage I do to myself by luxuriating in negative thoughts is one device I've used to help me eject them, and sometimes it works. But simply commanding them out of my head doesn't replace negativity with an uplifting and profitable experience. That's why I was particularly interested to see what Cayce had to say about ridding myself of frustration, hostility, and other negative attitudes.

One Basic Question, One Basic Choice

Though there are many negative attitudes in this life, how to overcome them, according to Cayce, is really one unified question. As human beings with free will, he says, we have one basic choice constantly before us: we can follow the way of God, or we can choose the path of rebellion. Choosing the way of God—following the example of the Christ consciousness within us—leads us to manifest in our lives qualities the Cayce readings frequently refer to as fruits of the spirit—such attributes as love, kindness, patience, gentleness, and cooperation.

Rebellion, on the other hand, turning a deaf ear to the godly impulses inside us, results in the opposite qualities: hostility, frustration, envy, and fear. If rebellion is what brings on these negative emotions, or at least makes us subject to them, then to lose them, Cayce tells us, we must instead choose God's way. According to the readings there are certain purposes, attitudes of mind, and specific measures that will help us to accomplish this.

Not "I Can't" but "I Will"

A major precept of the Cayce material is the power of the human will. This power is essential if we are to change the quality of our lives by overcoming negative attitudes. Some people might say, "I can't help feeling resentment; it's just the way I am." Or, "I can't help feeling frustrated. My life is so frustrating." To think that way about ourselves is to deny the power of will that is part of our makeup.

The readings affirm time and again that we *can* help it. We're not impotent lumps, mindlessly shaped by conditions around us. We can choose how we react to these conditions; we can use our will to decide what type of person we want to be, and we can make ourselves into that type of person.

Cayce expressed this rather poetically in reading 264–45, where he likened the person seeking an attitude change to a flower: "If thy inner self needs or requires attitude, then *conform* to same to be aware of that which grows and grows from within. Does the beauty of the rose come from that [which is] shed upon [it]? Rather does it grow from within. . . . So the awareness of . . . having the Christ Consciousness as they companion . . . is by *being*, by doing.'' Knowing that we have this power of will is prerequisite to using it. So the first attitude of mind we need in order to overcome negative emotions is self-confidence: the can-do attitude that a rose exhibits without even thinking about it.

Not that self-confidence is a snap to achieve—at least not for those of us not lucky enough to be born roses. First we must root out the causes of doubt if we are to build a true self-confidence.

The readings often told people seeking advice that they were experiencing a warring within themselves, and that this was causing disturbances in their minds and bodies. ''Confusions constantly arise . . . owing to the warring of one phase of the consciousness with another,'' is how this was expressed in reading 622–6. But who or what are the combatants in this war, what are the points at issue?

This warring results when an individual's spiritual purposes are not being adhered to by his mental attitudes and physical actions. This division of purpose eventually leads to doubt, and doubt in turn leads to fear. As explained in reading 538–33, the mechanism works like this: ''Fear is as the fruit of indecisions respecting that which is lived and that which is held as the ideal. Doubt is as the father of fear.'' And from fear can spring hostility, frustration, and a host of other negative emotions, what Cayce called ''dis-ease throughout the soul and mental body.''

The Power of the Ideal

Let's remember, when we talk about this "warring," that this is no harmless philosophical quandary; it can, for some people, be the source of excruciating pain. Nothing drove this home to me harder than the words of reading 2339–1: "Please explain why I seem to sob from within," Cayce's correspondent beseeched him.

The source, Cayce explained, was "frustration of ideals brought about by apparent circumstance, in which much of [what is] beautiful [within you] has been subjugated."

Once again Cayce reminds us of the power of the ideal—in this case the power it has to eliminate the warring within and to establish harmony by directing our physical and mental activities in ways congruent with our spirit's deepest sense of purpose.

For each of us, the ideal is the highest motivational quality we can conceive of and is closely related to our spiritual purpose in life. How important is it to know your ideal? According to reading 357–13, "The most important experience of . . . any entity is to first know what IS the ideal—spiritually." Once known, it can serve as a rudder to help keep our lives on a spiritually consistent course. Once the spiritual ideal is set we can use it to guide the thoughts and actions we adopt, which brings harmony to our purposes and actions on the physical, mental, and spiritual levels.

Knowledge of our ideal, then—plus that most important second step, dedication to it—will enable us to eliminate the warring within and overcome the negative emotions that result from it.

I can just hear some readers saying, as I did when I began my study of the readings, "It's fine to say that we should make all our purposes, thoughts, and actions conform to the best standard we can think of. But saying it and doing it are two different things. It doesn't sound so easy to me." Well, it isn't easy, and the Cayce material doesn't pretend that it is. But the readings do offer a message of hope in their constant assurance that we have an unlimited supply of help available. The help springs from the power of God and His infinite love for us, and is offered and made available through the example of Jesus.

In reading 2528–3 Cayce pinpoints this source of help quite explicitly, citing the words of Jesus. "Know in what you have believed," Cayce told a questioner who was suffering frustration, "and who is the author. Then live by it and live with it and you will find peace. . . . Be not disturbed, as He gives, because of frustrations. Know, 'I have overcome the world, and if you abide in me, I bring peace.' And peace is far from frustration."

Advice like this might give some non-Christians pause. Understandably, they might be reluctant to adopt a belief they consider the exclusive teaching of a religion not their own. But though the readings themselves are very stongly centered on Jesus, they also make it quite clear that membership in a Christian denomination is not a requirement for receiving the love of God or the guidance of Jesus. They are available to all of us through the examples Jesus set in his own life. More, the awareness of the abiding spirit of God—which the readings refer to as the Christ consciousness—is within every one of us already because we are all the product of, and a part of, the Creative Force: God.

By applying the Christ consciousness here as elsewhere in his teachings, Cayce amplifies his conviction that if we recognize that the principles of Jesus are within ourselves and always available to us, we can remain *constructively* aloof from the events and feelings that harass us in our lives. The idea is to fashion our own personal ideal through the guidance of the principles we discover within us—principles that, though exemplified by the life of Jesus, are above the narrow theological warfare that locks many of us from a creative acceptance of His spirit. In that way we can accept His radiant help without reference to specific creed or institutionalized religion.

The Frustration of Failure

Even those of us who are fully dedicated to our purpose in life can feel at times as if we are getting nowhere; our efforts can seem to be in vain. That must have been the situation correspondent 931–1 found himself in when he asked why failure brought on such an intense attack of frustration.

Rather than merely explain the source of frustration, Cayce offered his questioner a helpful perspective. "It is the 'try,'" he said, "that is the more often counted as righteousness, and not the success or failure." The poet Robert Browning felt the same way when he wrote, "Low aim, not failure is crime," or "a man's reach should exceed his grasp, / Or what's a heaven for?"

Cayce went on to encourage his frustrated correspondent with the words, "Failure to anyone should be a stepping-stone and not a millstone." In other words, don't be dragged into inaction by lack of success; see instead what you can learn from the experience and keep on trying.

When another correspondent asked directly, "Why do I feel so frustrated with life these past years?" Cayce answered just as directly, in reading 1703–3, "Lack of the peace and calmness within."

It's impossible for me to read about the need for inner peace and calm without thinking of meditation—a practice Cayce has recommended for so many varied purposes and problems. Meditation seems particularly suited to frustration because on a physical level alone it can be so calming. More than that, though, it is emotionally and spiritually healing by bringing us into closer contact with the Creative Force within. As Cayce put it in reading 281–13, "Meditation is emptying self of all that hinder the Creative Forces from rising along the natural channels . . . to those centers and sources that create the activities of the physical, the mental, the spiritual man; properly done this must make one stronger mentally, physically."

In addition, meditation reminds us of the goal of so much of our activity. "Hence as ye meditate," Cayce said in reading 1315–10, "as ye analyze thyself—it isn't . . . to be given the means so much as it is to assist and aid others that ye meet day by day to analyze themselves—that they keep away from hate, animosity, jealousies, fears; those things that produce disturbing forces in the lives of thy neighbor." The encouragement comes from being reminded of the good our work is intended to do, and that can go a long way toward making frustration bearable, if not get rid of it altogether.

Putting God's Power to Work

As we learn to awaken and manifest the universal love of God within us, say the readings, we become able to draw upon the unlimited power of the Creative Force. We become able to make use of this divine aid in our effort to overcome our negative attitudes—once we know it is available to us. Then, Cayce tells us in reading 2600–2, we can "put the burden on Him and it becomes light." We can call on Jesus, knowing He will cast our negative attitudes out.

Sounds simple, no? It may well be, but it definitely requires something more than asking. It won't work unless we ourselves do our part. The same reading tells us we must act in a way that is consistent with the divine love we are inviting into our lives. "But ACT in the manner as He did," Cayce instructs us, "not resenting any." We must treat our fellows in a way that reflects what the Christ consciousness has taught us; our behavior must set an example for them, offering it as a gift. "If ye put that resentment away, if ye put that doubt and that fear upon Him, He will cast it out; but thee, strengthen thy brethren. Teach, preach, talk to others." After all, we can't expect God to help us overcome our flaws if we insist on clinging to them in our thoughts and actions.

Cultivating Patience

One more attitude that will be invaluable in our endeavor to overcome negative emotions is patience: patience with our situation in life and patience with those around us, but more particularly patience with ourselves.

Cayce was concerned about the way frustrations can momentarily distort our capacities to think through and handle situations. In reading 2533–6 he told his questioner, "Frustration will at times cause, to this body, a reaction that becomes rather aggravating. . . . At the moment [the body] is too much disturbed to know the cause of same, but it blesses itself out . . . after same is passed."

Advice like this might lead some of us to think of patience as a passive quality, a matter of silent forbearance. Not according to the readings. It is, as described in reading 1968–5, a very active stance. "Learn again patience," Cayce counseled his questioner, "yet persistent patience, active patience. . . . Patience does not merely mean waiting. . . . Comply with patience' laws, working together with love, purpose, faith, hope, charity; giving expression to these in thy daily associations with those ye meet."

Thus patience becomes active by being the force that enables us to persist in our efforts, even though we might not immediately see their results. Most of us have quite a bit of work to do in getting rid of our negative attitudes. We can't afford to get discouraged with ourselves just because we're not instantaneously successful. We must keep trying, and patience is one tool that can help us.

Taking the Practical Steps

What we've been discussing so far are the purposes and attitudes of mind that form the essential groundwork for overcoming negative emotions. Now what we need are specific measures to take. What do the readings recommend we actually *do*?

One person who asked how to get rid of resentment was told just to "Chuck it out." Another, who asked how to overcome worry, was told, "Quit worrying!" Advice like that may seem simplistic, but the idea behind it is that we should never let ourselves become obsessed with the destructive attitudes we're trying to overcome; obsession merely feeds them. Rather, when we find ourselves falling prey to such negative patterns of thought as hostility or frustration, we should simply turn our minds elsewhere. As Cayce told his questioner in reading 294–91, "Fill the mind with something else!"

What this implies, of course, is that we have something positive to turn our minds toward. For Cayce, this something is divine love. He didn't just tell the questioner in reading 2600–2, "Chuck [resentment] out of your life," and leave it at that. "Let the love of God so fill thy mind, thy body," he instructed, "that there is NO resentment." If you let the love of God fill you, there will then be no room for anything negative.

Even that advice might not be specific enough for some of us, particularly when our minds are overwrought with bitter emotion. Cayce's advice was a lot more concrete when he addressed an Easter message to a prayer group back in 1941. "Let all so examine their hearts and minds as to put away doubt and fear," he said in reading 5749–13; "putting away hate and malice, jealousy and those things that cause man to err. Replace these with the desire to help, with hope, with the willingness to [share] with those who are less fortunate."

What we're hearing here is advice that we can *do* something about; attitudes that we can put into practice in our dealings with other people: ways, in other words, by which we can seek God's love and express it in our actions, "doing things that bring joy, harmony, peace in the minds and the hearts of thy fellow man," says reading 1641–1, thereby letting the light of God's love purify our own minds and our bodies. As Cayce expressed it, poetically but succinctly, in reading 987–4, "Turn thy face to the light and the shadows fall behind."

"Magnify Thy Agreements"

To apply this advice in human relations, many people were told to concentrate on the agreements between themselves and those around them, and to minimize the differences.

"In thy dealings with thy fellow man," Cayce said in reading 1765–2, ". . . seek first to find that which coordinates and cooperates. Magnify thy agreements and not thy discords. These will bring the greater influences and forces into the exeperience, enabling thee to make for the greater development."

This is not a matter of denying our differences; doing so won't change them. But we don't have to dwell on them. We can simply do our best to treat others as we would like to be treated, regardless of how much we disagree with them. Our disagreements do not have to color the way we act. "The trick," the reading concludes, "is to put all this into practice. It can be done!"

One way of magnifying our similarities is by recognizing the good—which in effect means recognizing the spirit of God—in the people we deal with each day. If we look for the God Force in others, which we know is there because it is in all of us, we can do a lot to eradicate hostility, Cayce promises. "When there is the . . . realization that the dealings . . . with its fellow man are only the meeting of the God Force . . . in those activities and lives of others," says reading 1217–1, "how indeed do they become as one—and how necessary that differences be not sought, those things that arise which bring fear, contention."

What Cayce would have us do then, when we find ourselves in conflict with others, is to remind ourselves that we are all a part of God because the Creative Force resides in all of us—and what greater thing can we all have in common, really, than our relationship to the First Cause of the universe?

As I write this, I keep pondering Cayce's emphasis on magnifying the virtues of others and minimizing their faults. My mind flashes back through the dozens of relationships in my life where I might have applied such an idea—and never did.

Going back to the seventh grade, I can still picture a classmate of mine whom I'll call Galen Mercer. At the time I called him the Prime Class Drip—which is what he remains in my mind even today. I remember the time he pestered me so much in class that I was forced to implant a sharp fist to his arm. (Since this was a Quaker school, where peace was the watchword, I found myself suspended for a solid week.)

I've never succeeded in magnifying Galen Mercer's virtues or in minimizing his faults; and in fact he is joined by a dozen other Prime Drips from my past: a football coach, a math teacher, a boss, and several others. Now, however, when I think of the time and energy I wasted stewing over these Drips I get mad at myself. Though perhaps I shouldn't; by doing so I am violating Cayce's precept that it is as bad to condemn yourself as it is to condemn others.

What I have learned to do, with the help of Cayce's ideas, is to put on the brakes when such perversely enjoyable thoughts come into my mind. It's purely a matter of applying willpower so far, and it hasn't been easy. But it is beginning to work. It's practical, and it actually helps. I'm beginning to be convinced that, if there's any role for vengeance in this world, it should be left up to the Good Lord.

Nip Hostility in the Bud

One important step in ridding your life of hostility is simply refusing to build it. One of Cayce's correspondents was concerned about his hostile treatment at the hands of the American Medical Association. He asked whether the sleeping Cayce thought their attacks on him would "come to naught."

"Depends upon the antagonistic attitude that the body assumes," Cayce answered in reading 969–1. "If ye would be antagonized, then be antagonistic! If ye would have peace, be peaceful!'' Turning the other cheek, reacting kindly even though we may be angry, enables us to build peace in our relationships with others and to find it within ourselves.

In fact, Cayce taught that antagonism can be melted by a quality the readings call "loving indifference," a concept I alluded to in Question 5. Loving indifference means acting lovingly ourselves, placing no expectations on the other person, and leaving the results in the hands of God. This seemingly contradictory phrase appears in reading 1152–2, where a correspondent asked what to do about a growing antagonism with a friend.

"This [loving indifference], to be sure, at first may be called contradictory,'' Cayce acknowledged. "For how *can* there be *loving* indifference?'' He suggested his questioner look to the life and words of Jesus for an example of how this is possible. Paraphrasing the words of Scripture, Cayce recalled how Jesus' followers "were called to His presence and they said, 'See, these in thy name heal the sick, cast out demons, yet they gather not with us. Rebuke them.' But what was His answer? 'Nay; nay, not so—for they that gather not with us scatter abroad the praises. Leave them, lest they turn again upon *you* and use that thou has done to thine own confusion.' ''

The attitude Cayce was recommending to his correspondent was, "LORD, THEY ARE THINE, AS I AM THINE. . . . I PRESENT THE PROBLEMS TO THEE. USE *ME*, USE THEM, IN *WHATEVER* MAY BE THY WILL IN THE MATTER.

"This then puts thee in that position that there is no stumblingblock, and that becomes the *loving* indifference. For ye have left it in the hands of the Creator, who alone can give life and withdraw it.''

Forgive and Forget

We don't always have the option of nipping hostility in the bud. Sometimes it arrives full-blown on the scene, or it's been developing slowly without our being aware of it. As might be expected, forgiveness is the recommended antidote for hostility that already exists.

In his book *In Tune with the Infinite*, Ralph Waldo Trine writes beautifully about the essential task of attunement with the Creative Force and of the power that comes from it, then speaks of its connection with forgiving: ''The great central fact in human life ... is the coming into a conscious, vital realization of our one-ness with this Infinite Life, and the opening of ourselves to this Divine inflow.''

Trine then speaks to the subject of hostility and forgiveness in a way that Edgar Cayce would surely applaud: ''Meet hatred with hatred and you degrade yourself. Meet hatred wih love and you elevate not only yourself but also the one who bears you hatred.'' In Cayce's terms, by forgiving we get to demonstrate the love of God to whoever is bearing us animosity, and through that demonstration we help him or her to become a better person.

But the readings don't stop at forgiving; they emphasize just as heavily going all the way to forgetting. Several people were told, as reading 1695–1 says, to ''leave off rather those inclinations to hold grudges. Let such experiences [of hatred or aggravation] be rather as not having been.'' Applying this advice is not easy, of course. It requires that we refuse to take note of temptations toward hostility, that we refuse to let them influence our thoughts and actions.

One specific step Cayce says we can take that will help us forgive and forget is to pray *thankfully* for others, acknowledging their good points. According to reading 1304-1, it's impossible to pray with ''prayers of thankfulness . . . and still hold a grudge or a feeling of animosity.'' When we pray this way, Cayce explains, we are recognizing that the other person is ''at least attempting—in [his] own way—to be of help, whether in a feeble way or in whatever way. For all power that is in the hands of man has been *lent* and . . . is of God.

''Thus when individuals hold a grudge they are fighting the God within themselves against the God within the individual . . . towards whom such [grudge] is held.'' Given Cayce's understanding of the nature of mankind, it's clear that when these forces collide—your hostility on the one hand; your recognition of the God within your ''nemesis'' on the other—they cannot coexist and it's your hostility that will give way.

Overcoming Selfishness

Negative attitudes of all kinds have their roots in selfishness. Cayce was very clear about this in reading 987-4: ''What is ever the worst fault of each soul?'' he asked rhetorically. ''SELF—SELF!

''What is the meaning of self?

"That the hurts, the hindrances are hurts to the self-consciousness; and these create what? Disturbing forces, and these bring about confusions and faults of every nature.

"For the only sin of man is SELFISHNESS!"

Cayce couldn't have been any clearer than that: We feel we have been hurt, so we adopt an attitude of hostility. We want more from life, so we feel frustration. The logical implication is that if we can overcome selfishness, we can eliminate the negative emotions that arise from it.

The key here is not to *deny* the self, but to use it to express God's love; to use it as a way of expressing your personal ideal and to fulfill the real purpose of your life. In reading 262–24 Cayce assured his questioner that God's "grace is sufficient." By that he meant that if his questioner always remembered that God—or God's expression in the Christ consciousness—was always with him, there would always be "that constant, prayerful attitude for a purposeful life; forgetting self, preferring another above self"—focusing on the good of others rather than on selfish goals—which is the ultimate meaning of Cayce's counsel to "Lose self in Him" and thereby banish negative emotions.

Said simply, through the power of our will, we can replace negative attitudes with the desire to help others.

The message found throughout the Cayce material is that we get out of life exactly what we give. "As ye forgive, ye are forgiven," says reading 2600–2. "As ye love, so are ye loved. As ye resent, so are ye resented."

But we can give out only what we have within. Thus

there are two parts to a general program for overcoming negative attitudes:

First: we must build within ourselves the positive attitudes of love, self-confidence, dedication to our ideal, faith in the love of God, and active patience.

Second: we must share the fruits of these positive attitudes with others. "Not," as Cayce says in reading 1537–1, "because it is ennobling, but because it is RIGHT in THY sight!"

To replace our hostilities with peace, we must bring peace to others.

To overcome our feelings of frustration and discouragement, we must encourage others.

To find love, we must simply love.

QUESTION 7

How Can I Overcome Feelings of Guilt and Fear?

Many psychoanalysts agree that the root cause of neurosis—and often a consequence of neurosis as well—is guilt and fear. They are among the most powerful termites eating away at a healthy ego and a tranquil life.

One of the most effective tools for removing guilt is the capacity to forgive yourself—whether you are actually guilty of something or not. Self-forgiveness is as strong a tenet of Edgar Cayce's teachings as it is of psychoanalytic theory, but it's also another one of those concepts that are so much easier to talk about than to put into practice.

Analysts attack guilt and fear by probing the unconscious mind for hidden traumas—bruising incidents from early childhood that have planted guilt trips in the area of our mind that Freud called the superego, where they remain to screech at us our whole life long. By bringing these traumas to the surface, where they can be examined by the conscious mind in the cool light of reason, therapists hope to loosen their hold and set us free.

Cayce's model of human consciousness was quite different from that of Freud. As we learned in Question 1, Cayce saw the inner life as divided into three levels of consciousness: the conscious, the subconscious, and the superconscious—this last, the superconscious, being the area that has access to the divine. Unlike the analysts, Cayce would have us handle guilt and fear by steering us toward harmony with the divine, with the Creative Force that was once our mooring line and from which the human spirit has drifted.

Cayce is not alone among the world's thinkers in feeling that the roots of guilt and fear can be traced to our separation from God, the First Cause. The great Danish philosopher Kierkegaard declared in the nineteenth century that fear came to man because of this separation, because human beings have set the satisfaction of physical urges as our top priority, over our connection with God. The result of this choice is guilt, which adds not only to our fear but to our self-hatred.

No matter whose theories you subscribe to, the sad truth is that guilt and fear consume a tremendous amount of energy that could well be used for building a genuinely better life. If we can return to the source that put us here, say both philosophers, the chances of throwing guilt and fear out the door are immeasurably enhanced.

Worry Only Hurts

So often the energy we waste is expended in the form of worry. We immerse ourselves in worry as part of a desperate search for something to *do* about the fear and guilt we are suffering, which is why some have called worry "the soulmate of fear." No wonder worry was so well represented in the letters that filled Edgar Cayce's mailbag.

Cayce was adamant in his responses about worry: Far from helping, it can do serious harm. "The body should not allow worry, or uncertainty, to bring destructive elements into the physical being," he said in reading 550-3, "for worry will not correct conditions; neither will taking extra thought bring that to pass that is already set." Worry, in other words, won't alter the course of history, but preparing yourself for the future might. "Rather make thine self in the way of being equal to whatever may present itself . . . ," Cayce continued; "for in this there will be found the better condition to meet these exigencies that arise, and the physical body will respond."

Even more explicit about the physical consequences of worry was reading 338–9: "If there are the worries and aggravations," the reading says, "these . . . will reflect in the functioning of the organs of the central nervous system and blood supply."

Anyone who's ever sat fuming over dinner and developed a case of heartburn knows Cayce was right about this. And if you've suffered from ulcers, heart attack, or stroke, you've probably heard your doctor give similar advice. But if we're not to worry, what are we to do?

The *short* answer, according to Cayce, is to pray. "As much as practical, leave off worry . . . ," he said in reading 760–31. "Why worry? For worry only makes

matters worse. PRAY rather than worry. He answereth
prayer.'' So basic to Cayce was this advice that, in
reading 3569–1, he created a little maxim and reinforced
it with humor. ''Remember the injunction—never worry
as long as you can pray. When you can't pray—you'd
better begin to worry! For then you have something to
worry about!''

Prayer lay at the foundation of the advice Cayce
extended to a concert pianist who faced ruin because of a
fear he could not handle. The reading is 3509–1. ''My
career as a pianist was brought to a end,'' the man wrote,
''through my extreme nervousness and lack of confidence, and other talents have suffered because of an
overpowering fear. What am I to do?''

''Right about face!'' Cayce ordered. ''Know it is
within thee! Defying this has brought the fear, has
brought the anxieties. Turn about, and pray a little
oftener. Do this several weeks—let a whole moon
pass . . . ye will be surprised at how much peace and
harmony will come into thy soul.''

If you've got a skeptical streak in you as I do, you
might be saying at this point, ''Pray your troubles away,
huh? That's pretty familiar advice. But what makes
prayer more than a distraction? What makes it a constructive act?'' To find Cayce's answer to that, to understand
the specifics of what he would have us do to overcome
guilt and fear, we have to look more deeply into his
explanation of who we are and how we function.

A Unified Approach to Health

The Cayce readings deal quite specifically with how to overcome such negative emotions as guilt and fear, but unlike psychoanalytic theory, they take an approach that can only be described as "holistic." The readings approach mental and emotional healing in the same way they deal with physical healing—by coordinating and harmonizing all the dimensions of an individual's life: the physical, the mental, and the spiritual.

From the perspective of the readings, it's quite impossible to heal only part of a human being; the entire spectrum of human experience must be addressed. Healing mental attitudes such as guilt and fear involves the mental condition, certainly, but it also must involve the individual's physical activities and spiritual health for the healing to be total and sustaining.

To understand the perspective on attitudinal healing offered in the Cayce readings, we first must grasp the full picture of who we are physically, mentally, and spiritually.

Who We Are, Who God Is

We are, according to the readings, essentially spiritual beings who are experiencing temporary incarnation in the physical world. At our core, at our spiritual center, we have the same will and desire as the Creator of the universe because in fact we are a part of the Creative Force, or God. And yet, as souls created by God we have been given the divine gifts of free will and a creative mind. Out of all of creation, Cayce tells us, we alone have the power to defy the will of God if we so choose. Our free will empowers us to direct our creative mind in any direction we wish, creating crimes or miracles. It's all up to us.

Free will, however, does not make us invulnerable. We may be able to build thought forms that are not in accord with the will and nature of God, but we pay a price for doing so. Not that some thunder god will point a finger at us and zap us the way Zeus zapped Prometheus. God, residing inside us, doesn't have to punish us from without; rather, the price we pay is discord and unhappiness within our very selves, because at our spiritual center we *are* a spark of God—a portion of the Creative Force. Discord naturally results when we act contrary to the nature of the Creative Force within us.

What then *is* the essential nature of this Creative Force? Cayce tells us what Jesus did: that God is love— unconditional love. The desire of God, says Cayce, is to nurture, help, and support all of creation. At our own spiritual core we have the same nature, we have these same desires, because we are in fact one with the Creator. But because we have free will and the power of a creative mind we can—and we have—developed identities that have very different natures and desires. *That,* according to the readings, is the true root cause of fear and guilt.

But the readings also reassure us that we are all on a path of spiritual evolution. Through the vast dimensions of time and space, over the great journey of lifetimes from incarnation to incarnation, we are learning to awaken our will and to align it to the will of the Creator. That, you may remember from Question 2, *is* the essential purpose of our lifetimes—our current incarnation and the others we may experience.

The great teacher in this ultimate lesson is life experience—what you might call trial and error. And the law behind life experience is cause and effect. The Bible refers to this law as "sowing and reaping"; the Eastern religions call it karma. Really, it is all the same. What both the Western and Eastern traditions affirm is that we live in a lawful universe. Fear and guilt are born of the law of consequences in that they are the consequence of "errors" in attitude or action. Because fear and guilt are the result of errors, they can be healed by the same law that created them.

The Only Sin

According to the readings there is really only one "sin" or "error," and that is selfishness. Our true spiritual nature, flowing as a natural consequence of our being a part of the Creative Force, is to be selfless, to be as filled with unconditional love as God is. When we go against this impulse and instead concentrate only on self, guilt and fear naturally arise. Logically then, we should find joy, peace, and freedom from fear when we become truly more concerned for someone or something beyond just ourselves.

Cayce said this with startling bluntness in reading 540–11: "Worry more about somebody else than you do about yourself, and you'll be a lot better off."

He was just as explicit, and even more concrete, in response to an obviously troubled questioner who asked,

"How can I overcome fear of advancing old age and being alone?"

"By going out and doing something for somebody else," he answered in reading 5226–1; "that is, those not able to do for themselves, making others happy, forgetting self entirely. These are but material manifestations but in helping someone else you'll get rid of your feelings."

Remember Who We Are

Another key factor in eradicating fear is remembering our true identity. According to Cayce's description of the universe, as living parts of the Creative Force we are the children of a loving Creator—a Creator who knows us, who cares about us, and who abides with us always. He abides with us because He is always within us, making His presence felt whether we respond appropriately to it or not. This awareness of His presence can have a profound impact on our ability to face life with courage and fearlessness. For example, this awareness can awaken in us one of the greatest weapons we have against fear—a sense of humor.

Cayce made this point plain in reading 5302–1 when a correspondent asked how to overcome fear. Cayce's counsel: "By seeing the ridiculous and yet the funny side of every experience. Knowing and believing in whom ye have trusted, in the Lord; for without that consciousness of the indwelling, little may ever be acomplished."

In essence, then, according to the readings fear is the result of our own willful separation from God, the source of all love and life. The purpose of this separation is often a preoccupation with selfish, ego-centered concerns, what the readings often term self-indulgence or self-aggrandizement. Consequently, the healing of fear is through the reawakening of our oneness with this source of love, plus the willingness to be used as a channel through which that source can reach out in compassionate service to others.

The readings often cite the life of Jesus as the perfect example of compassionate concern for others, and of the power of selfless giving as a healing tool.

"Fear is the root of most of the ills of mankind," Cayce pointed out in reading 5459–3, reminding us that this fear can take different forms in different people, "whether of self, or of what others think of self, or what self will appear to others." However that fear feels to the individual, the proper course is to "fill the mental, spiritual being with that which wholly casts out fear; that is, as the love that is manifest in the world through Him who gave Himself [as] the ransom for many." If we make it our goal to do as Jesus did, to use our concern— and our efforts—for others as a way of manifesting the Creative Force's love and concern, our reward will be that "such love, such faith, such understanding, casts out fear."

Guilt and the Power of the Ideal

Hugh Lynn Cayce, in his fascinating book *Faces of Fear,* notes that guilt is caused by a lack of love for self and others, and that the resulting conflicts we experience are caused by our not living up to our ideals. "For to remove guilt we first have to forgive ourselves," he wrote, "which can only come about if we do start living up to our ideals."

Guilt, after all, is just another word for self-condemnation. It strikes us when we feel we have failed to live up to a personal standard or ideal and then condemn ourselves for that failure. To heal feelings of guilt it's not enough just to want to feel better about ourselves; we've got to assess our behavior, recollect our ideals, and understand why the two are not working in harmony. Hence, the readings say, there are four keys to understanding and healing guilt.

First, we must realize that guilt is tied up with preconceived notions of success or failure. We sometimes think that an isolated experience is the final determiner of whether we have succeeded or failed. The readings, on the other hand, promise us that we never fail as long as we keep trying.

One correspondent never used the world "guilt," yet it's clear from his question that he was condemning himself harshly. "How have I failed to use wisely what God has given me?" he asked. "Why am I so confused about so many things?"

The sleeping Cayce saw just what his questioner was doing to himself: "Do not—do not feel that ye have failed," he cautioned. "Do not judge self. You have not failed *yet*. You only fail if you quit trying. The trying is oft counted for righteousness." To bolster his questioner's courage and faith in himself, Cayce reminded him of the words of Jesus. "Remember as He has given, 'I do not condemn thee.'" If Jesus would not condemn the questioner, Cayce is saying, why should he be condemning himself? Instead, "Go, be patient, be kind, and the Lord be with thee."

A second contributor to self-condemnation can be the tendency to condemn others. A principle often expressed in the readings is that we get back what we give out. In the folk idiom we say, "What goes around comes around." Speaking biblically, we reap just what we sow.

In terms of guilt, this is true because, in the perfect lawfulness of the life experience, our attitudes toward others determine our attitudes toward ourselves. If we hold resentments toward others and refuse to forgive, these same emotions and attitudes can turn inward. This is just what Cayce meant when addressing a woman who asked, "Why do I feel responsible for the whole affair, and responsible for the future?"

"Because there has been a great deal of resentment builded by implication, by the body...," he explained in reading 316–1. "Hence there are those periods then, with the thinking or meditating over the past, the resentment is turned toward self!"

A key step in overcoming guilt therefore is learning to forgive others so we can learn to forgive ourselves. "Do not condemn self!" Cayce implored her. "Rather make self's life one of service to an *ideal*, and leave the whole in the hands of the Creative Forces that rule the destinies of every soul!" What she needed to do was to manifest the love of the Creator in her daily life by practicing forgiveness. After that it was out of her hands; in common parlance, at that point she had to "Turn it over to the Father," she had to "Let go and let God."

A third factor in removing guilt is, simply, taking action. Self-condemnation can be the result of *not* doing what we know we *should* be doing. Ironically, sometimes we may perpetuate guilt because we prefer it to actually getting up and doing something to manifest our ideals. In that way, guilt can actually be the child of laziness. We may be so familiar with our old companion guilt that we may be more comfortable feeling it than challenging ourselves to live up to our ideals.

We should never fool ourselves, says reading 307–13, that inaction can be a route to real comfort, "For there cannot be a full mental and physical expression where the mental *continuously* condemns self for *not* doing [what] it knows to do—and excuses it in one way and another!

"Either fit the self to be the channel through which [what] it believes may [be expressed], or don't express that's what you claim to believe."

Pretty harshly stated, it seems to me, but by his advice Cayce is trying to save us from a double-headed monster: the ravages of guilt, and the undermining error of hypocrisy. Even worse than not acting in accord with our beliefs is trying to take credit for them when we won't put them to use in our life.

The fourth and final step in eradicating guilt is believing in the forgiveness of the Creator. Many of us refuse to. Many who struggle with guilt are carrying an image of God as wrathful and judgmental. We may have picked up this notion in any of a number of ways—perhaps we have some inner need to believe it—but the readings insist that God is loving and forgiving.

If we can develop a more forgiving vision of the Creator, the readings promise, we can open ourselves to the healing power of grace. And the personal experience of grace can in turn motivate us to become channels of grace to those we meet, more fully putting our ideals into action. As we channel grace and blessing to others, as we live in accord with our spiritual ideals, we erase fear; we erase guilt; and we build into our eternal selves treasures that are imperishable.

QUESTION 8

How Can We Know the Will of God and the Nature of Free Will?

Edgar Cayce removed one impediment to my acceptance of God by not requiring that I picture Him anthropomorphically: no white beard and frock coat; no bushy eyebrows waggling furiously at my misdeeds. Instead, he refers to God as the Creative Force, letting me picture a universe filled with universal divine energy. And yet, Cayce believed God to be a personal God, one we can relate to closely; in fact, Cayce often suggested that we can meet God face-to-face within our inner selves. Furthermore, though God may not take a human form, though He may not operate according to the rules of human psychology, one of Cayce's clearest teachings is that God does have a will and that it is our proper goal to harmonize with it.

For centuries philosophers and theologians have argued over the existence and nature of will—God's and man's. How can it be possible, they asked over and over, for God to be all-powerful and all-knowing and for man still to have the power of volition? How can man's actions possibly be freely chosen if God has the power to see all of the future and all of the past; if God has, in effect, *designed* the future and the past, designed all of existence?

To someone not lucky enough to have full religious faith, that word "design" can be the key to a clearer picture (and a readier acceptance) of the notion of God's having a will.

When Rabbi Herbert Weiner and Presbyterian minister Dr. Richard Drummond jointly wrote their article "How Do We Determine the Will of God?" for the A.R.E. magazine, they introduced the idea of a design for creation this way:

"I don't question that God has a will," Weiner wrote. "I think there is a will in the universe. This universe represents a design, something which in a sense was foreseen and planned. . . . Therefore it is not difficult, as in some Eastern faiths, to say that one should try to put one's will in harmony . . . with the basic will of the universe. I think there's will for the ordering of nature."

This point of view suggests that if there is a grand design of creation as reflected in the obvious order we see in nature, it doesn't matter whether we call it God's will or simply the natural consequences flowing from the order that was created by the First Cause that put everything in motion. We can most likely find our best contentment by seeking to know that grand design, and by joining in with nature in that design.

Supposing an architect were to design a house. He would take into careful consideration all the different elements that go into the finished building. But if a building contractor fails to follow the architectural design, he'd be more likely to end up with a monstrosity than a mansion. What Cayce suggests, as we'll see as we explore his words about God's will and man's, is that we are in effect building contractors for God; our task as co-creators is to help build His mansion according to his awesome perfect design. If, as the Bible suggests, "In my Father's house are many mansions," we would do well to construct our own edifice in harmony with the grand design.

Somehow the word "design" seems so much less formidable than "will" that, for some reason, I find it more comfortable, perhaps less threatening. But obviously the meaning is the same, and that's what counts. With that perspective in mind I have been able to read Cayce's words on man's will and God's and evaluate them in relation to my own life.

Free Will: Our Birthright

That human beings have free will was a basic assumption in many of the Cayce readings. He called it an "attribute" of our souls, but by that he meant far more than just some incidental quality our souls have. In a sense it is a *defining* attribute, one given to us at the moment of our souls' creation. Will, he said in reading 1129–2, is the "birthright to each soul from an All-Wise Creator" who would never take it away from us, but whose wish was that "no soul shall be separated from Him." Rather, we were meant to use our will as a way to "find our place in *His* oneness."

Right here at the outset Cayce has separated his notion of the soul and its actions from those who believe in total predestination. What actions we take in the material world are completely within our control. Even the effects of heredity and environment, those supposed ultimate determinants of all human behavior, can be subject to the power of individual will, he claims.

"As to what an entity does concerning its environs or hereditary influence . . . ," Cayce said in reading 274–1, "this is governed by the action of the will." Here he made clear how essential an attribute of the human soul will is by calling it "that active principle making for the *individuality* of an entity." More than a mere quality of the soul, it is "the whole development of an entity." It is what makes our souls unique, Cayce believes, and what sets them off from the Creative Force itself.

In fact, not only are our actions not predetermined, they and their outcomes are not even known to God until we take them. "Having given free will," he explained in reading 5747–14, "then—though having the foreknowledge, though being omnipotent and omnipresent—it is only when the soul that is a portion of God *chooses* that God knows the end thereof." It is our free will alone, in other words, that is the ultimate shaper of our destiny.

At first reading this sounds like an impossible contradiction: God, an omnipotent force whose desire it is that we unite with Him, grants us a gift through which we may draw away from Him; God, an omniscient force, grants us a gift by which the outcome of our actions are not known to Him until we commit them. Is this in fact contradiction, or does it somehow follow from the very nature and purpose of that gift?

The "Individuality" of the Soul

When Cayce spoke of the human will as being the thing that gives us individuality, he meant more than just the unique characteristics of our personality, those qualities that make my thoughts, feelings, and actions different from my neighbor's—though clearly will does play a major role in shaping personality. But Cayce's words were precisely chosen. He spoke of will as making for the individuality of an "entity" because, according to his view of creation, will is what separates us in consciousness from the ultimate Creative Force we call God.

Here's the definition of will Cayce gave in reading 262–81: "What, then, is *will*? That which makes for the dividing line between the finite and the Infinite, the Divine and the wholly human, the carnal and the spiritual." Without will we would be unconsciously a part of the Creative Force, but we would also be totally without this individuality.

There is a second consequence, though, of this individuality resulting from free will, and it is part of what makes free will a "gift" in Cayce's eyes. Without will, Cayce has said, we would be like automatons. With it, he said in reading 1435–1, "we become as the children of the Father." Not that a will-less state would be totally without beauty; in fact, we would be "as nature in its beauty—but ever *just that*." We would be no more or less beautiful than the golden trees on an autumn mountainside. We could never grow beyond that beauty. But *with* free will, "the soul of man may grow to be equal with, one with, the Creative Forces." That is why Cayce calls free will a gift.

That is also what makes free will, in Cayce's estimation, such a powerful tool. Even in the face of astrological forces—forces that, while not predictive or determining, Cayce believed to have a strong impact in the human sphere—free will prevails. In addressing the influences affecting a fifty-four-year-old woman who wrote to Cayce for advice back in 1931, he said in reading 2673–1, "While these [astrological] forces appear, and innately give many an urge to an entity, there is *no influence* beyond the *will* of an entity." Free will is stronger than any other influence, Cayce asserts, for, by separating the entity from "a universal cosmic consciousness" free will also gives the entity "capacities to make itself, its will, one with the Creative Forces . . . , using same as constructive forces in that direction, or becoming at variance with the Creative Forces—bringing discontent, disorder."

We all have latent urges, Cayce believed, and we all have manifested abilities, virtues, and faults. But free will is the thing that lets us decide which of these urges will come to life in action, which of our abilities we will develop and use, which of our virtues and which of our faults will hold sway in our daily decisions. What Cayce is acknowledging is the power of choice.

Choosing "Oneness"

So the use of free will boils down to making choices. Cayce suggests several times through his readings that we have before us good and evil. We must make our choice. Of course, most of us learn only through hard knocks and bitter experience what choices to make—or rather, what choices we *should have* made.

The Cayce scholar Violet M. Shelley, writing in the A.R.E. book *Face to Face,* said, "It is one thing to acknowledge that our free will is our inheritance, our birthright, and quite another thing to realize that we use or abuse this gift constantly in the choices that we make. The choice of thought, attitude, action and speech is present every waking moment. The decision is ours as to whether those choices will make us the worthy companions of the Creator. . . . As man's desire is, so is his destiny."

What this says to me is that though life might be the tide that sweeps us along, our own will is the rudder, so it's a good idea to keep a strong hand on the helm. And it wouldn't hurt for God's hand to be on the helm to help us navigate safely. In Cayce's language, this means aligning our will with God's, choosing oneness with the purpose of the Creative Force and rejecting self-indulgence. Either course is available through the exercise of free will.

Cayce's ideas in this area bring up an apparent paradox that I find intriguing. By surrendering your will to God's, you gain much greater freedom: freedom from fear, from despair, from frustration. But as they say in the carnivals, "You pays your money and you takes your choice." Cayce suggests that you are better off if you do not make choices that serve only yourself, and according to the testimony that filled the bulging A.R.E. mailbags, a lot of people have found this very satisfying advice in the long run.

But the key question remains: Even if we want to make these "proper" choices according to Cayce, can we? And if so, how? How do we get ourselves to change?

You don't need a psychic *or* a psychoanalyst to tell you that people don't change easily. A look at the billing records of any modern psychotherapist will tell you that even people who *want* to change their lives do so slowly and with difficulty. But then, psychoanalysts believe that change comes only through insight. They maintain that we must first come to understand how our personalities were formed—usually a pretty lengthy process—before we can go about making them different. Cayce says we can change through an act of will.

In fact, Cayce said in reading 1129–2 that inertia will prevail, that the desires in life are continuous, "unless they are acted upon by the will of the entity in regards to [its] relationships . . . [with] the Maker." This strikes me as a basic and fundamental element of Cayce's conception of the nature of man: Will is what allows us to make changes in what have become automatic patterns in our lives. Even more, "changes *only* come by the activity of the will." And the Cayce promise, according to reading 1210–1, is that whoever makes the will "one with those Creative Forces or constructive influences may build and *build* and BUILD!"

Whether this belief puts the Cayce teachings in conflict with the practice of psychotherapy, or whether in fact the two perspectives can be joined and seen as one, will have to be up to the reader to decide. I know only that there is testimony on both sides: the thousands of letters that have flooded the A.R.E. offices from people praising the way Cayce's advice has changed their lives, and the untold number of therapy patients who insist their lives are better for the insights they've gained. Who knows for sure? Perhaps it was through psychoanalytic insight that these patients finally learned to exercise free will and lead their lives in accordance with the natural design of the universe.

Am I Doing the Will of God?

The will of a stubborn child can be exasperating—sometimes to the point of parental frenzy. When a child sets his or her will up against that of its parents, the parents know that what they want the child to do is for the child's own good. But sometimes nothing they say can convince the child of that.

Frequently, the Cayce readings imply that we are like that child: We don't realize that our stubborn will is blocking the way to a more harmonious life. Most of us have learned from experience that if we go around stamping our feet and demanding, "I want this," and "I want that," our free will can make us pretty unpopular with our peers. But throwing temper tantrums is not the only way of being stubborn. All we have to do is refuse to listen to counsel, such as Cayce's implied promise of the reward that will be ours if we change our attitude of wanting things only for ourselves and instead work for better things for others.

Many of those who *have* made that commitment, who have taken a deep breath on the diving board and made the decision to turn their will over completely to the will of God, report an invigorating plunge. They express a sense of contentment, reactions that range from relief all the way to euphoria. The members of the first A.R.E. study group all shared such a reaction, prompting them to write in the second volume of *A Search for God*, "Happiness is found in the mind and heart of those who without thought of self seek to know the way of God."

The basic thrust, then, of Cayce's advice is for us to recognize the power of our will, but to keep in mind the importance of utilizing it for the development of our soul, which is the essential and enduring center of our deepest consciousness. It is for that purpose that Cayce tells us to get with the Creative Force that put us here, to line up with it and accept it wholeheartedly. To do that, we must continually search for what this great will is and learn the best way to join with it.

Looking for the Telltale Signs

The readings state categorically that there are certain qualities—justice, mercy, and love, to name a few—that are clearly in line with God's will for us. Cayce's prediction is that material advancement not based on these qualities will eventually come to ruin. He even claims that we can verify this for ourselves. "Look into the hearts of those that are apparently successful in material things," reading 531–3 says, "and unless such successes are founded in the spirit of justice, mercy, love, and long-suffering and brotherly kindness, they must fade and fall away." On the other hand, if our successes *are* "builded in the fruits of the spirit, they find pleasure . . . in the eyes and heart of your Maker."

It strikes me that Cayce is not necessarily promising us

monetary reward, but there are more kinds of success in this world than riches. In any event, what's clear is that he is naming qualities that anyone with common sense can see are "builded in the fruits of the spirit" because they are the exact opposite of selfishness. Guide your actions by these principles, Cayce seems to be saying, and at least in those actions you will know you are conforming to the will of the Creative Force.

Now, that's all well and good when our choices and motivations are clear. But life isn't made up exclusively of obvious choices. Most of our decisions are more complex than that, or at the very least our motivations are harder to figure out. How can we be so sure we're conforming to God's will in those situations?

That was the quandary faced by a fifty-year-old woman back in 1941, prompting her to ask Edgar Cayce, "How may I know when the will to a course of action is justifiable, or when I am forcing my own personal will?"

"By the listening within—there is the answer," Cayce said in reading 2174-3. "For the answer to every problem . . . is ever within—the answering within to that real desire, that real purpose which motivates activity in the individual." What Cayce wanted her to listen to was that famous "still small voice within" we talked about in Question 1, the voice of the Christ consciousness that Cayce said resides within each of us and steers us toward our real purpose in life, rejoining with the Creative Force. Listen to that voice, is Cayce's advice. It will affirm our actions if they are properly motivated, because "each soul knows within when it is in an at-onement."

Three years later another woman asked a very similar question: "How can one be sure that a decision is in accordance with God's will?'' This time Cayce spelled out in more detail the steps to take in consulting with the still small voice.

First, he said in reading 2072–14, ''Ask self in the own conscious self, 'Shall I do this or not?' The voice will answer within.'' In other words, first apply your consciously learned standards. Hold the proposed action up to the light of reason. See what your conscious mind tells you. ''Then meditate, ask the same, yes or no. You may be very sure [that] if thine own conscious self and the divine self [are] in accord, you are truly in that activity indicated.'' If the still small voice that speaks to you in your meditation agrees with your conscious decision, then go for it!

Similar advice, but this time recommending prayer instead of meditation, was given to a woman in reading 3250–1. ''In thine own mind,'' Cayce said, ''decide as to whether this or that direction is right. Then pray on it, and leave it alone. Then suddenly ye will have the answer, yes or no.'' But that's not the end of it. Cayce suggests a double check.

''Then, with that yes or no, take it again to Him in prayer, 'Show me the way.' And yes or no will again direct thee from deep within.

''*That*,'' said Cayce, ''is practical direction.''

It doesn't surprise me that Cayce would give such similar advice resting on meditation and on prayer. Both have often been said to be communications with God: prayer being talking to Him, and meditation listening. Nor does it surprise me that he should tell us to listen to the Christ consciousness within us. If that was his advice for discerning the true purpose of our life, naturally it would apply to the task of discerning God's will.

In fact, Cayce took the final step by recommending that, if we want to live our lives in conformity with God's will, we should pattern our lives after the life of Jesus. The real question we should ask ourselves is, "What would Jesus have me do?" not simply, "What shall I do?" Jesus, remember, was according to Cayce the perfect example of selfless giving, the perfect example of attunement with the Creative Forces. If, through the processes of meditation, prayer, and conscious deliberation, we can determine that our course is one Jesus could have lived with, we can be pretty sure we're on the right track.

Cayce offers one last test, the proof of the pudding so to speak, of whether our actions are in accord with God's will. Apply what you think is God's will, he advises, and that very act will deepen your understanding of what God's will truly is. "As you apply God's love, God's light," he said in reading 262-5, "so does understanding come of what God would have each of you do day by day."

I'm not sure just how this understanding is supposed to come to me, whether by some psychic means or by intuition. But it seems reasonable to me that if the actions I take are harmonious with the natural order of the universe, I will naturally feel their "rightness," and that will be enough to spur me to further actions in that direction.

There's a New Testament verse, Romans 8:31, that has received considerable circulation: "If God is with us, who can be against us?'' And really, if God is omniscient and omnipresent, how can you find fault? But when we apply our own will to the purpose of putting ourselves in alignment with God's will, the thought might better be expressed as, "If *we* are with *God*, who can be against us?" If our own will is taking action to make sure it is aligned with God's, then we become a participant on the scene, a co-creator with God, rather than a mere spectator.

As far as Edgar Cayce was concerned, we could hardly do better than that.

QUESTION 9

Is There Life after Death?

There just might be as many different kinds of fears as there are people. In a survey of young adults, Edgar Cayce's son, Hugh Lynn, listed sixty-two different fears. The survey results revealed five that were among the most often experienced by the group: fear of failure, fear of meaninglessness, fear of rejection, fear of war, and fear of loneliness. Other fears prevalent in other age groups run a wide gamut: fear of poverty, sex problems, failing health, pain, impending doom, and loss of loved ones are merely a few. But the most fundamental, universal, and frequent fear, running across all age groups, is the fear of death. It is hard for us even to imagine the loss of our own individuality and existence. What could it possibly be like not to exist? What happens when we are gone?

Obviously, belief in life after death would be a reassuring answer to this fear. But I've never been one to believe in something simply because it would reassure me. My experience as a journalist, as well as the basic

nature of my personality, both impel me to explore and
assess answers, not just accept them.

On the assumption that you, the reader, also hunger for
a rational exploration, not just a pep talk, let me tell you
of the journey I took that eventually convinced me—
though only after great doubt and hesitation—that survival beyond death is a certainty.

On Madison Avenue they have a definition for it:
"Death is nature's way of telling us to slow-w-w-w
down." We may laugh at jokes about death, but we laugh
grimly, because the truth is we start dying the minute we
are born, and we know it. There have been some interesting developments lately in physics, psychology, medicine, parapsychology, and theology that suggest death
isn't quite the ogre we've been taking it for, but our
personal enlightenment in this area comes slowly, sometimes with reluctance.

One of the problems has been terminology. There are
certain words and phrases, created in an age when people
wore togas, not Jordache jeans, that are not inviting to
the modern mind. Such ancient phrases tend to turn off a
mind used to thinking of moon shots, space shuttles,
DNA, computers, and Concorde jets.

Some people, for example, think that *spirit* sounds
spooky; they may find *consciousness* more appealing.
Soul sound ominous to some; *extended self-awareness*,
though, can convey the same meaning. *Heaven* sounds so
exalted and unapproachable that it seems forever out of
reach; *extra-physical existence*, it seems to me, would
throw up less of a roadblock to the modern mind.
Whether these are exact synonyms or not, I've learned

that, for me, they are much more capable of taming the nasty fear that pops up each time the idea of death does.

The problem lies with both science and religion. Science has brought us a whole new vocabulary. But it has tended to supplant religious concepts rather than supplement them. At the same time, religion has clung to medieval words and images that simply don't communicate or convince the way they used to.

The Age of Science came in on a tidal wave that bypassed many islands. Things that couldn't be conveniently measured were left to dry in the sun. There are signs now, however, that science is looking back over the islands to see what it has missed—including the possibility of life after death. There are also signs that theology is not as averse as it once was to a rational, scientific exploration of the *evidence* of life after death. The two supposedly opposing camps might be moving toward some points of agreement. But meanwhile, in between the two camps is the perplexed individual who really doesn't know what to believe. Science has put a dent in his faith, and he's still staggering under the impact.

One early example of movement on the part of organized religion is a study conducted a half a century ago by the Church of England. Mediumship had come into fashion in World War I England, where the daily lists of casualties from the trench warfare in France had become so overwhelming that the population sought desperately to find comfort; they did not want to think that their sons and brothers, dead on the battlefields, were gone forever.

When the Church of England first announced its plans to study whether communication with the deceased was possible, it was widely expected it would condemn the work of mediums as contrary to biblical teachings. Surprisingly, while the church's final report could offer no reassurance that there was evidence the soldiers did live on, the Archbishop of Canterbury and his associates did come to the conclusion that psychic phenomena were not in conflict with church teachings; rather, they were an evidential complement to them.

I know that the research I eventually did into the subject of survival acted not as a deterrent to religious belief but as a strong reinforcement and complement.

My First "Encounter" with Ghosts

Long before I came across the works of Edgar Cayce, I researched a story that turned out to be instrumental in overcoming my skepticism about survival after death. At the time, though, I knew little or nothing about things paranormal, so I approached it with journalistic caution.

Late in 1972 an Eastern Airlines jumbo jet, Flight 401, went down in the Florida Everglades. Both the pilot and the flight engineer were killed. Shortly thereafter, crew members on several sister ships reported seeing the deceased pilot and engineer on board their own planes. Not the kind of wispy, unsubstantial forms often associated with ghosts, but apparitions that looked solid and vividly real, as if they were there on the planes in person. Whatever they were, these ghosts were benevolent. The sightings stopped after a few months, but only after some senior pilots literally performed exorcisms on the planes where the ghosts were most often seen.

Now, I had always considered ghosts as suitable only

for fiction—Hamlet's father, *The Turn of the Screw*—or for kids out on a Halloween romp. At best they were a subject for theologians, whose faith I found admirable but not easily transferrable to an age of material science.

Given the perspective I had at the time, what I set out to write was a book about how a jet-age ghost story could possibly be created and believed in these enlightened times—in other words, the origins of a modern myth. But the deeper I got into the research, the more I realized that these reports could not be lightly tossed aside. The deceased captain had appeared and disappeared in the first-class section, right in front of several passengers and crew. The full shape of the flight engineer had materialized in the lower galley, instructed the crew to check a malfunction, then vanished. These and other warnings and messages all proved to be exactly correct. In all, nearly two dozen of these strange and startling events were reported. Slowly, the research for the book began shifting from an analysis of a modern myth to an inquiry into the rational possibility of life after death.

This was a switch I wasn't quite expecting. But then, at the time I wasn't aware of the many other serious investigations that had been done. By the time I sat down to write *The Ghost of Flight 401* I knew much more. And by the time I finished researching the book that followed, *The Airmen Who Would Not Die*, about the crash forty-four years earlier of the British dirigible R-101, I was able to open the book with the following words:

"On the evening of March 12, 1928, there was set in motion a long chain of events that has brought many discerning, and even skeptical people to the inalterable conclusion that there is life after death. After months of research, I had to agree that I had become one of those people who were convinced by the evidence.''

Let me share with you some of the serious scientific inquiries that helped move me, skeptic that I was, to such a conclusion.

Learning to Make Un-common Sense

Had I been aware, at the time I began my research into Flight 401, of the study conducted by G.N.M. Tyrrell, a sober and reputable British physicist and mathematician, I wouldn't have been so surprised that my jet-age ghosts were uniformly described as looking as solid as you and I. The majority of the sightings he explored exhibited the same phenomenon: apparitions that obscured the background, making them look decidedly *un*ghostly.

Tyrrell examined 130 such cases of apparitions, all of which had appeared when more than one person was present to witness the scene. His final conclusion, reported to the British Society of Psychical Research, was that "over a hundred cases represents too large a number to be dismissed out of hand." Further, he reminded his fellow researchers, "Subjective hallucination is too easy an explanation."

Tyrrell suggested adopting an outlook on such research similar to the one I eventually came to. Common sense, he felt, should be suspended. After all, "The best of modern science deals with un-common sense."

At the time I began my own research, Dr. Elisabeth Kubler-Ross, the highly regarded professor of psychiatry at the University of Chicago, had been deeply into the study of terminally ill patients for two decades. It was her work that first brought to the attention of the general public the idea that dying people must go though preparatory stages in order to finally accept their own death. By now her book, *On Death and Dying,* has become the standard text for people who provide care for the terminally ill.

But it was her courageous statement about survival after death that startled the scientific community. She stated flatly that her lengthy study of patients who have clinically died, then been brought back by emergency medical intervention, "will confirm what we have been taught for two thousand years—that there is a life after death."

Several years before, Dr. Kubler-Ross had gone through a remarkable experience. For some time she had been considering giving up her specialized work. One day a woman entered her office, and Kubler-Ross immediately recognized her as a patient who had died several months earlier.

"The patient said she knew I was considering giving up my work with dying patients, and that she came to tell me not to give it up," Kubler-Ross told a *Chicago Tribune* reporter. "I reached out to touch her. I was reality-testing. I was a scientist, a psychiatrist, and I didn't believe in such things."

To further test the incredible situation, Kubler-Ross had the woman write a short note and later had the handwriting analyzed. Both the note and the signature matched the handwriting of the dead patient exactly. Dr. Kubler-Ross has kept that note under glass since then. "It came at a crossroads," she says, "where I would have made the wrong decision if I had not listened to her.''

But this was only one case. Over the years, Dr. Kubler-Ross collected data from all over the world on patients whose vital signs had stopped but who had been brought back. A number of elements persistently turned up as common to all these so-called near-death experiences: movement through a long, dark tunnel toward a brilliant, comforting, joyful light; being greeted and encouraged by some old friend or relative who had already made the same journey; an instant replay of the person's whole life, as if the events were being projected from color slides; the awareness of being in a body, but a different body from the physical one they had known.

Later, Raymond Moody, M.D., collected 150 cases like these and published them in his celebrated book *Life after Life*. In fact, his cases so closely matched those of Kubler-Ross that she gladly wrote a foreword for his book, even though her own book on the subject was yet to come out.

This unexpected concordance of similar incidents eventually brought both Kubler-Ross and Moody, at separate times, to see Dr. Karlis Osis, the psychologist heading up the American Society of Psychical Research. As medical scientists, neither Kubler-Ross nor Moody had been familiar with the extensive probes conducted by the ASPR in this field.

When, in the 1960s, a Gallup poll showed that 73 percent of Americans accepted the concept of life after death as a reality, Osis had set out to explore the question on a larger scale. He queried a total of seventeen hundred physicians and nurses in the United States and India about their deathbed observations; over half the data was collected using an exhaustive sixteen-page interview form.

The stories Osis collected were remarkably similar to those reported by Moody and by Kubler-Ross. I won't go into all of the details here, but there were two features that I found particularly convincing. "The apparitions that appeared in two-thirds of the reported cases," Osis says, "wanted to take the dying person away to another modus of existence, by calling, beckoning, demanding." A careful scientist might theorize that these beckoning figures were mere hallucinations brought on by the patients' brains being affected by disease. The contrary proved to be the case. "People with these medical factors saw *fewer* apparitions which wanted to take them away," Dr. Osis reports. "People who were clear-brained saw *more* such figures."

The second convincing aspect of Dr. Osis's findings is that, despite the cultural and religious differences between the United States and India, the cases were still strikingly similar—just as Dr. Kubler-Ross has found in comparing her U.S. findings with those from Australia. What these two factors convince me of, therefore, is that these experiences are more than figments of the imagination, and that they are not the product of cultural conditioning. They are not experienced only because we are taught to experience them, nor because we desperately want to.

Dr. Kubler-Ross sums up her work by saying, "People describe their deaths as a way to shed their physical existence like a butterfly [emerging] out of a cocoon. Beyond a shadow of a doubt, there is life after death." Dr. Moody concludes his observations with: "If experi-

ences of [this] type . . . are real, they have very profound
implications for what every one of us is doing with his
life. For, then it would be true that we cannot fully
understand this life until we catch a glimpse of what lies
beyond it."

Thanks to the serious scientific inquiries I've researched—
the ones described here and many others—I have come to
believe that there definitely is something beyond death to
catch a glimpse of. What form it takes, what the meaning
and qualities of such experiences are, I still have no firm
idea, which is why I was curious to learn what answers
Edgar Cayce offered to these questions.

On the Other Side of the Door

Edgar Cayce regarded death as simply a move through
what he called "God's other door," just another step in
the process of soul development that continues until we
achieve oneness with God. This soul development, you
may remember from Question 2, is really the ultimate
purpose of our life, according to Cayce. Reincarnation,
in his scheme of things, gives us the opportunity to
continue that development on the earth plane by providing us a lifetime in which to act in accordance with
God's will. But it is only in between earthly incarnations,
from the vantage point afforded by a whole other plane of
existence, that we are able to perceive our soul's development up to now and assess what work still needs to be
done. Or we may discover, during this period of "astral
education," that in fact we no longer need to be earthbound.

But what is it like to pass through this door? What,

many correspondents asked Cayce, are some of the planes we pass through "on experiencing the change we call death?"

When asked this question in reading 5749–3, Cayce explained that when we die, we go through a process very similar to the one we experienced when we were born here on the earth. We had little consciousness at our moment of birth. Our awareness of life emerged slowly, through babyhood and childhood, as we worked our way through a long learning process. Our death, according to Cayce, brings us through a similar experience on the spiritual plane. So in this sense, death is simply a birth into another plane.

Actually, Cayce gave a number of different descriptions of what it is like to make this transition, some of them poetic, others directly informational: "The passing in, the passing out, is but the summer, the fall, the spring; the birth into the interim," he said in reading 281–16. What it is *not*, he stressed in reading 136–18, is "passing away, or becoming a non-entity." Instead, he explained in reading 989–2, "A death in the flesh is a birth into the realm of another experience, to those who have lived in such a manner as not to be bound by earthly ties. This does not mean that it does not have its own experiences about the earth, but that it has lived such a fullness of life that it must be about its business."

One question that occurred to many of Cayce's correspondents was just what elements this surviving spirit is composed of. Cayce answered in reading 900–34 that when we lay aside the physical body, the thing that "in the physical [plane is] called the soul becomes the body of the entity, and that called the superconscious"—the part of our consciousness that, during our earthly life, has access to the divine—becomes "the consciousness of the entity."

But as to what *form* the spirit entity takes on, that's not so universally predictable, apparently. "It takes that form," he answered in reading 900-19, "that the entity creates for itself in the plane in which the existence has passed."

Now, I can't honestly say I can picture just what choice of forms Cayce is talking about, or how that process works. But it seems to me that the explanation of how the mind creates an entity's form after death lies in reading 3744-4, where he said, "FOR THOUGHTS ARE DEEDS, and are children of the relations reached between the mental and the soul. . . . What one thinks continually they become; what one cherishes in their heart and mind they make a part of the pulsation of their heart." This is in complete agreement with Cayce's premise, discussed in several earlier chapters, that the "mind is the builder," however that is actually accomplished.

One thing on which Cayce and the general scholars of the paranormal seem to agree is that once we move into the astral plane, life may look little different from the world we've known. According to many mediums, some persons who have died suddenly, feel they are still living on the earth plane. They have to be encouraged by mediums to break the bond and move on to pursue their soul development.

Cayce, when asked if death instantly ended all feeling of the physical body, or how long such feeling would last after death, answered in reading 1472-1, "This would be a problem; the length of time is dependent upon the way in which unconsciousness is produced in the physical body or the manner in which the consciousness has been trained to think about death.'' So here again the death experience is in part created by the mind during life.

As a side point in the same reading, Cayce furthered the case for survival after death by citing the experiences of mediums. ''That there is continued consciousness is evidenced, ever, by the abilities of sensitives [mediums] and the like.'' Then, in answer to the reading's original question, he concurred that we may die and not immediately realize it: ''As to how long [death may take], many an individual has remained in the state called death for years without realizing it was dead! The feelings, the desires for what are called appetites, are changed, or one is not aware at all.'' The one thing we can count on, though, is that ''the psychic forces of an entity are constantly active, whether the soul-entity is aware of same or not. Hence, as has been the experience of many, deaths become as individual as individualities or personalities are themselves.''

The Landscape of the Afterlife

The picture of a soul not recognizing the death of the body it had inhabited raises intriguing questions in my mind. The old-fashioned image of heaven, complete with golden trumpets and clouds of singing angels, would call attention right away to the fact that you had gone through ''God's other door.'' So if consciousness does live on, what kind of real estate, what kind of geography, could this physically disembodied mind live in and still make sense?

The late H. H. Price, a renowned scholar who was an emeritus professor of logic at Oxford, has provided a possible answer for this "What Kind of Next World?", a chapter he contributed to Eileen Garrett's book *Does Man Survive Death?* "If the 'other world' is a spatial one," he asked. *"where* is it?"

Price suggests an answer to his own question by examining the stuff that dreams are made of. Here is a space of a different kind, and yet when we dream, everything appears just as real as the space of everyday life. "Both for good or for ill," Price said, "our dream experiences may be as vividly felt as any of our waking ones, or more so."

So the geography of the afterlife is there, this theory suggests, and it's boundless, though no real estate agent can buy or sell it, and no armies can fight over it. During sleep, the unconscious mind already shows evidence of visiting this real estate, which has streets, houses, trees, fields—everything that the physical world has. It simply represents a different kind of space, where we would meet people (as we do in dreams) and communicate (perhaps by telepathy, since we rarely hear audible voices in dreams)—all of it very real and vivid, just as dreams are. And since the geography of dreams is plastic and expandable, it could handle an infinite number of deceased, with no overcrowding or housing shortages!

"It would of course be a psychological world and not a physical one," Price pointed out. "It might indeed *seem* to be physical for those who experience it. The image-objects which compose it might appear very like physical objects, as dream objects often do now; so much so that we might find it difficult at first to realize we are dead.''

The late William Ernest Hocking, for years the Alford Professor of Philosophy at Harvard, joined H. H. Price in recognizing the importance of dreams as a clue to an afterlife, feeling that their three-dimensional reality could provide for a spatial geography beyond our own. ''The event of death,'' he said, ''involving the body of the self belonging to one nature system, does not necessarily involve the death of the self.... Death may thus be relative, not absolute. And the transition in death, a mental transition, [is] devoid of distance.''

The rationalist ideas of Professors Price and Hocking, combined with the findings of Dr. Kubler-Ross and other researchers of the near-death experience, made it possible for me to conceive that we can move into another world when we die, and that there would be plenty of rather realistic space to move around in. The individual mind and its sense of awareness could exist under these theories, and a body at least as real as the one we have in our dreams could serve it.

It is this conception of the afterlife that I think of when I read Cayce's words in reading 5756–4: ''The physical world, the cosmic world and the astral world are one—for the consciousness, the sensuous consciousness, is as the growth from the subconsciousness in the material world.'' Whether Cayce would have accepted that our dream landscapes bear relation to the landscape of the afterlife, I don't know for sure. But even the most rationalist of psychologists would agree that our dream life is a ''growth from the subconsciousness,'' and in that respect would accept Cayce's oft-repeated premise that "the mind is the builder."

Communicating through the Door

I find it interesting that Edgar Cayce, acknowledged as the foremost psychic of his time, did not act as a medium in the conventional sense. Not that he didn't believe such communication was possible. In the reading cited earlier, in which he discussed how long it might take for an individual to recognize its own death, he made specific mention of the "abilities of sensitives." And in fact there were occasional incidents in which Cayce used specific discarnate entities as communicators.

Cayce even had a meeting with Eileen Garrett, the medium who drew worldwide attention when she communicated with the airmen of the downed dirigible R-101. At their meeting, Cayce and Garrett performed cross-readings that were particularly illuminating, demonstrating the power of psychic phenomena.

Garrett, a pragmatist with a keen intellect in addition to psychic abilities, worked with the staid British and American Societies of Psychical Research as well as with Oxford, Cambridge, and Columbia University. Her work fortified and helped to explain how Edgar Cayce could accomplish his unbelievable feats. (This was the period when Cayce's medical readings were capturing the attention of the press.) But her work differed from Cayce's in that it focused on demonstrating that individuals continue to live on in full awareness of themselves after they have moved into the astral plane, and that we can establish communication with them.

Cayce felt this communication was of limited usefulness because the deceased entities in the astral plane (or "borderland" as he once described it) are not developed enough spiritually—in fact they are often "earthbound" —and are thus unable to provide high-level spiritual guidance and inspiration. Death, after all, does not necessarily bring immediate spiritual enlightenment. Instead, Cayce preferred to reach directly for the Creative Forces, where the greatest store of spiritual guidance resides.

Nonetheless, Cayce accepted the evidence of messages received through reliable mediums. He believed, in fact, that everyone is psychic to a greater or lesser degree, since everyone's superconscious is interconnected. In the course of the reading in which he acknowledged the abilities of "sensitives," he expressed concern that "the ability to communicate . . . disturbs and worries others." He tried to calm the fears of many puzzled letter writers who were startled by spontaneous experiences of telepathy or clairvoyance. Even today the A.R.E. does considerable work reassuring such people that their psychic experiences are quite commonplace and not symptoms of psychological disturbance.

What I find reassuring is the agreement I see when I study the material produced by both these twentieth-century mystics, Cayce and Garrett, plus the reports of the clinical experiments performed by the various societies dedicated to psychical research. Over and over the same themes recur about the quality of existence after death. There seems to be a welcome relief from stress and physical suffering, but the need apparently continues for spiritual and mental development. That development, according to both Cayce and the work of mediums, is directed toward gathering spiritual knowledge and expanding the capacity of love—goals very similar, you might remember, to those cited by Theodor Reik as the end purpose of psychoanalytic treatment.

Werner Heisenberg, one of the most respected physicists of the twentieth century, whose Uncertainty Principle shook the foundations of modern science, once said about the exploration of the unknown: "The positivists have a simple solution: the world must be divided into that which we can say clearly, and the rest—which we had better pass over in silence. But can anyone conceive of a more pointless philosophy, seeing that what we can say clearly amounts to next to nothing?"

My own inquiry into the spiritual unknown began with the exploration of a jet-age ghost story, back when I could conceive of such an incident as nothing but a myth. What I ended up with were some rather firm intimations of immortality. As an investigative journalist, I didn't feel quite so far out on a limb when I discovered the work of Kubler-Ross, Moody, and the others who examined the evidence with a healthy, if benevolent, skepticism. Their work, I saw, was without fuss or incantation, and yet it was saying some terribly important things. And that allowed me to open myself to the words of Cayce and other mystics in a way I never would have before.

The fear of death dominates many people, and I can't say I'm totally without such fear. But my inquiry so far has led me to the firm conclusion that survival after death in some form is a certainty. Such a conclusion can't help but have a tremendous impact on our lives. And with that impact comes considerable comfort and reassurance that the loss of loved ones is not final by any means.

As to the loss of myself? My own eventual death? I can only hope that by the time my turn comes, I will be able to say, as Teilhard de Chardin did: "Why should I be afraid of death, since it is only a mutation, a change in state?"

QUESTION 10

What Religion Reveals the Greatest Truth?

I can never forget the Reverend Dr. Joseph B. C. Mackie, minister of the Northminster Presbyterian Church in Philadelphia when I was a boy. He had all the proper credentials, out of Princeton Theological Seminary, and commanded the pulpit with his burly physique, his handsome face, and a resonating voice that seemed powerful enough to shatter the elegant chandeliers that hung from the vaulted ceiling. With every sermon he scared the living daylights out of me. (He also sent me scurrying to the dictionary, along with his son Joe, to look up words like *fornication*. We both delighted in finding such naughty words printed there for all the world to see.)

Dr. Mackie didn't speak from the pulpit; he thundered from it. He got his points across, there's no doubt about that. How could I forget such phrases as, "Fear the Lord thy God. He is a jealous God!" In the balcony behind Dr. Mackie three stout alto and soprano ladies would burst into hymns that blasted sin, extolled the virtuous, and made everyone feel about six inches tall.

By the time services were over I would stumble out of church wondering what I, a deflated little sinner, was doing in this world. I remember looking up into the sky one time on my way home and literally wanting to scream: "Stop the world! I want to get off!"

Later, at Quaker school, things eased up a little. At least there I felt free to put together a do-it-yourself kit of religion. But this takes a lot of practice, and I'm not sure I've mastered it yet.

Although comparisons are supposed to be odious, I've never been able to resist comparing religions. One result is that I've found myself envying those who can settle comfortably into a spiritual niche—envying them, that is, except when they point judgmental fingers at others who have found different niches they are content with.

A devout Christian of any denomination who lives up to the ideals of Christ deserves the greatest of respect, it seems to me, as does any Jew or Buddhist or Muslim who lives by his or her traditions. In fact, the same is true for the faithful of any of the world's great religions. On my forty-day trek from Kathmandu to the base of Mount Everest I had the chance to observe closely the profound Buddhist faith of the Sherpas. There in their remote mountain villages on the roof of the world, far from supposed civilization, they lived the most spiritually civilized lives I have ever seen.

Armed with these experiences and perspectives, what has impressed me in my research on Edgar Cayce is the way his words reflect the unity of all faiths. Because of his stout conviction in the oneness of everything—physical, mental, and spiritual—a commonality is established among all the religions of the world on which mutual respect can be based.

* * *

Although Edgar Cayce was steeped in the Judéo-Christian traditions, his respect for all the religions of the world was equally devout. When asked by his correspondents how they should regard people with different beliefs, he answered unequivocally, ''Be merciful and kind to those of any faith,'' as he did in reading 254–87.

The explanation of this position goes beyond a mere live-and-let-live attitude. Using a botanical metaphor, the reading challenges Cayce's questioners to recognize that no single answer suffices for all needs: ''Are there not trees of oak, of ash, of pine? There are the needs of these for meeting this or that experience. Hast thou chosen any one of these to be the ALL in thine usages in thine own life?

''Then, all will fill their place,'' the reading continues. ''Find not fault with ANY, but rather show forth as to just how good a pine, or ash, or oak, or vine, thou art.'' Your business, in other words, is to attend to your own spiritual development, not to judge the spiritual paths of others, and to demonstrate your own development in the way you treat your fellow human beings, setting a spiritual example for others. Moreover, according to Cayce it is instructive to seek out the *essence* of truth wherever it might be hiding, regardless of the name it goes by. By looking for the one truth everywhere, we remind ourselves that the One God is the umbrella over all creation, and in the process we just might learn something about our fellow man and about ourselves.

It's no surprise, therefore, that Cayce would warn his listeners against the prejudices that have scarred religious history. ''Lean upon the arm of the divine within thee,'' he said in the same reading, ''giving not place to thoughts of vengeance or discouragements. Give not vent to those things that create prejudice.''

The theoretical underpinning to this advice—a familiar one to us by now because it is so central to the Cayce tenets—is set forth in reading 3179–1: "Remember that the greater service to the Father-God is the manner in which one treats the fellow man, for this is the manner in which one treats one's Maker." As Cayce said in reading after reading, with each and every soul a creation of and co-creater with God, how we treat our fellows is exactly how we treat God.

Carrying this theory one step further, Cayce reflected on the separations that have grown up between religious organizations, and on how unnecessary—or even harmful—they can be. "This in itself," he said in the same reading, "should convince anyone of the senselessness of denominationalism."

This is a recurring theme in Cayce's work, one that lies at the heart of many of his answers to life's questions: that whatever separates one man from another also separates us from the Creative Forces of the universe—from God. "The Christ . . . died for ALL—not for one!" he reminded us in reading 3976–27. "No sect, no schism, no -ism, no cult!"

This issue, of prejudice and division, must have troubled Cayce's mind greatly; he stressed it often, speaking forcefully of its dire consequences not only for our spiritual development but for human suffering here on our planet. "More wars," the reading continues, "more bloodshed have been shed over the racial and religious differences than over any other problem! These, too, must go the way of all others; and man must learn—if he will know the peace as promised by Him—that God loveth all who loveth those who love Him, whether they be called this or that sect or schism or cult!''

I personally find that wording remarkable. Not ''God loveth all who love Him,'' but rather ''God loveth all *who loveth those* who love Him.'' We should, as I understand this, be always aware that the practice of any religion—no matter how different from our own—is still based on love of creation, on recognizing the unity of all things. We should love one another for the spiritual impulse we all have in common, not hate and fear one another for our divergent ways of conceptualizing and expressing that impulse.

Edgar Cayce's ecumenical views extended well beyond the various denominations of Christianity; beyond even the different religions of the Western world. He was able to blend the faiths of the Far East with his profound belief in the Judeo-Christian culture.

The reason Cayce could accept this blending is contained in reading 443–3. When his correspondent asked, ''Which is the highest teaching for this entity, the Christian or the Oriental?'' Cayce answered, ''These should be one, for their sources and their emanations . . . are toward the same source.''

Asked by the same questioner what the true ideal should be for measuring religious belief, Cayce replied, ''Only that which answers to that within self can to that soul be the true ideal.''

There it is again: our old friend and ultimate spiritual yardstick, the personal ideal. Establish that, then measure your behavior and beliefs—of whatever kind—by it, and you will be on the path of truth.

Fascinating to me—though not surprising—is the fact that this cross-cultural respect is a two-way street; true masters of the Eastern spiritual tradition hold the principles of Jesus in equal esteem. And as we'll see, their esteem rests on the same foundation, that practice and belief are truthful if they are true expressions of the believer's inner self.

Although Cayce probably was unaware of him, a Western scientist named Baird T. Spalding conducted a tour of fellow scientists through India. He summarized the results of his tour in four small volumes titled *Life and Teaching of the Masters of the Far East*. These illuminating volumes demonstrate the parallels between Eastern and Western spirituality, echoing Cayce's thinking.

In the fourth volume of his works, Spalding writes, "One does not gain mastery or illumination by going to India and sitting at the feet of a master. One gains mastery by listening to the deepest facets of his own nature and by obeying what he learns there. . . . All the power of the universe is back of every high motive, every true impulse that stirs in man's inner nature . . . This is the manner of the masters and their instruction is always that you must be true to the self. Live the life of the self, express what is inherently true until you are outwardly what you inwardly long to be."

Here, in a few brief sentences, are both a revealing introduction to the philosophy of the East and a concise summary of some basic Cayce teachings. Listen, through meditation and prayer, to the truth as it expresses itself in your personal ideal, and you will be certain that you are acting in accord with the highest creative principles.

The key, I think, to the concordance between Cayce's teachings and those of the Far Eastern masters lies in what one pundit told Spalding: "When Christ spoke, 'These and greater things shall ye do,' . . . [He was] speaking of the only true unity, the soundness of the individual and his relationship to and with the whole."

Anyone, Spalding concluded, can live this life of the masters, this "life of oneness . . . if he will drop his alliance with institutions and religions and races and nations and accept the alliance with the universe." Exactly the advice that Cayce gave his correspondents, and the Eastern explanation is strikingly similar to Cayce's as well.

"All separation is purely a matter of individual hypothesis," Spalding wrote. "One cannot really be separated from the whole for he is created within it, is a part of it. . . . Love is the great unifier in the consciousness of man. . . . When one's nature expands in love he will sooner or later find himself in a loving attitude toward all, and in this attitude he not only lifts himself but all those around him into that same oneness."

Since the ecumenical spirit of Cayce embraces not only all religions but science as well, and because I am by natural inclination drawn to science, I find it interesting to note the points of contact between Cayce's teachings and the learnings of modern science. Not that science should be considered a religion. But there are important connections between what the two disciplines have to say about the oneness of everything in existence.

Fritjof Capra, in his book *The Tao of Physics,* comes

up with a sharp observation about this. Capra points out that at first the concept of solid objects seemed shattered by atomic physics when it was demonstrated that everything we see is composed of smaller elements. But quantum theory, which Capra holds to be the highest peak of modern physics, has brought us around full circle. "Quantum theory . . . ," he writes, "reveals that basic oneness of the universe. It shows that we cannot decompose the world into independently existing smallest units. As we penetrate matter, nature does not show us any isolated 'basic building block,' but rather appears as a complicated web of relations between the various parts of the whole. . . . We can never speak about nature without, at the same time, speaking about ourselves." This, clearly, is a scientific understanding of reality that is in harmony with Cayce's cosmology.

Though Capra doesn't use expressions like "God within us," he does say that explaining nature just means showing its unity. Further, he says that when we move from the realm of matter in physics into the realm of consciousness in mysticism, we discover a "different reality behind the superficial mechanistic appearance of everyday life."

Capra sums up by saying that "science does not need mysticism, and mysticism does not need science. But man needs both."

Cayce, I suspect, would have nodded in agreement, then taken the assertion one step further: Man, he might have said, *is* both.

EPILOGUE

Impact on the Author

No guidance, regardless of its intrinsic truthfulness, is of any practical value unless it can be made use of by its readers. As I struggled to understand the importance of Edgar Cayce's words, most of them spoken more than half a century ago, I realized that there was only one way I could know whether his guidance has any relevance to people today: I had to ask them. What resulted was a little questionnaire, sent to over a hundred members of the A.R.E., asking how Edgar Cayce's answers to life's ten most important questions had influenced their lives. The responses I got, from people all over the United States, from people in all walks of life and from many different backgrounds, formed the cornerstone of my acceptance that the Cayce readings could indeed have an impact on citizens of the second half of the twentieth century.

And then it struck me: I'm a citizen of the twentieth century too. After tracing Cayce's influence on such a wide cross section of people, it seemed fitting that I should recount the results of my own quest, casting aside my journalistic reserve and revealing the personal.

A task like that is awkward for me, perhaps because I'm so used to hiding behind the dispassionate mask of detachment we journalists assume as we forcibly dig out the most personal information from other people. But it would be only fair, I decided—and probably good for me—to make the attempt, to give myself a taste of my own medicine by, in effect, giving myself an intensive interview. I present my answers here in the hope that they will afford you some perspective on what the Cayce material can mean to a "benevolent skeptic" like me.

Question 1: Has Edgar Cayce established or reinforced the belief that God exists? If so, how?

I have to admit that Cayce has clearly reinforced my belief. It existed before, but at rather low voltage. Now I find that Cayce's concept that the Creative Forces of the universe are manifestations of God makes it possible for me to conceptualize God as an omniscient, omnipresent pool of infinite energy that can be drawn on in a personal, direct way at any time.

It has become easier for me to conceive of opening the self up to this divine inflow to let it permeate every cell of the body, which creates at least a psychological infusion of energy that becomes almost palpable and can at times result in physical energy. There is, at times, a sense of "refueling," so to speak. I also find, in visualizing this, that there is a sense of personal comfort and relief in "letting go"—turning myself over to a higher power.

Because Cayce pictures God as merged with the physical, mental, and spiritual anatomy of each entity, rather than as a detached anthropomorphic figure, there is no longer a sense of separation, and I can picture God as truly personal and within me.

Question 2: Has Edgar Cayce helped determine your purpose in life? If so, how?

Cayce placed considerable emphasis on setting an ideal to define our purpose in life. Although I have had difficulty with this, others have reported great success. As a result of culling the Cayce material, however, the idea of ''getting with it'' (that is, getting in tune with the universe) has turned out to be helpful to me since I am a somewhat timid explorer of the vast cosmic domain. I have never been able, as Margaret Fuller was, to flatly ''accept the universe.'' I suppose my resistance can be ascribed to stubbornness, ego, and other aspects of bullheadedness.

I have now become able to set the ideal of getting into attunement with the universe and find it surprisingly beneficial. Through Cayce's benign influence I have been able to set a regular time each day to meditate about this—which is not as easy as it sounds. But in doing so I find myself able to make a smooth shift into the cosmos without grinding gears. If there is one factor in meditation that stands out, it is the self-command to ''BE STILL.'' When I forcibly bring myself to that screeching stop, it's amazing how minor problems and distractions automatically lose their abrasiveness. I had not been able to do this before. Cayce's admonitions about impatience have been helpful here. They have smoothed the way by making it possible for me to aim toward a harmony with the cosmos instead of fighting it with futile kicking and scratching. With this attunement as a long-term goal, I find the difficulties of daily living easier to put up with. I still feel the urge to grab the wheel of *Spaceship Earth* at times. But this urge has gradually weakened. I'm more able to sail with the wind instead of fighting it.

Question 3: Has Edgar Cayce helped you find peace in a turbulent world? If so, how?

My answer to this question flows from my answer to the previous question. By turning over to God and the cosmos decisions that are beyond my control, I am better able to put up with those things that are beyond my control and to work toward changing those things I *can* cope with.

It's hard for me to admit that there are things happening in this world that are beyond my control. This is, of course, a ridiculous posture to take. The proper task is to clearly define those happenings that we can do something about, and work on them constructively. If we take action on these, then we can justifiably say to hell with the turbulent world around us and replace futility with action.

Cayce's philosophy has been of considerable help with this. If we can get out of ourselves and turn our attention to other people, the ego is considerably relieved. I see in Cayce's work a wonderfully clear road map. The problem that remains is learning to follow it. He prescribes a course of both acceptance and action that offers a way out if we can.

* * *

Question 4: Has Edgar Cayce helped you toward better health and energy? If so, how?

I find that this is true in many subtle ways. Through Cayce's reminder to strictly follow a regime of moderate exercise and sensible diet each day, I have found a source of detectable fresh energy and better body tone. Almost everybody realizes the need for exercise. It is simply the reminder to give this a high priority that helps me override the tendency to procrastinate. Cayce has prompted me to start each day with exercise in spite of other pressures that seem more important at the time. This priority on exercise seems to pay off in how I handle all the other jobs that come up later in the day.

The same principle is true as far as diet is concerned. I can't study Cayce without becoming more conscious of the importance of watching my diet. In becoming more conscious of this, it becomes easier to discipline myself to bypass the tempting junk foods and reach for the more nutritious vegetables instead. Cayce's diet recommendations were well ahead of their time, yet they are simple enough to utilize easily.

Very important to me has been Cayce's stress on holistic health and healing routines. These were also laid down well before today's recognition of their value. Through meditation, and by visualizing the body at optimum functioning, from the tiny cells up through the larger organs, many ailments are measurably relieved, even if the mechanism is undetected by the conscious mind. Both physical and emotional problems can be helped in this way, as several schools of modern medicine now recognize.

*   *   *

Question 5: Have you been helped to work and love at your highest capacity? If so, how?

Since these qualities have been stated to be the end objectives of psychoanalysis, they are worth special attention. Some people have spent years in analysis—not to mention a heavy bankroll—to gain these objectives. Cayce offers a less arduous and less expensive way to do the same thing. Having experienced both methods, I think I can say that Cayce's way is at least equally efficacious.

In general, psychoanalysis ignores the spiritual side of living, and thus leaves a large gap. To work and love at the highest level is bound to involve the entire being. This includes the physical, mental, emotional, and spiritual.

To work and love at our top level we often need to be inspired, and inspiration is more often than not a spiritual quality. By reaching for contact with what Cayce calls the superconscious, the element of consciousness that has access to the divine, we are more likely to experience a more selfless love, a benign love that embraces others as well as ourselves. Cayce's recognition of the reality of the spiritual dimension gives him a marked edge over the finite and limited Freudian outlook.

Question 6: Have you been helped to overcome frustrations, hostility, and negative attitudes? If so, how?

If there is any one question I've had the most trouble with, it is this one. I have an uncommonly strong urge to luxuriate in getting steamed up about certain people I dislike. I perversely enjoy collecting injustices and mulling them over in my mind. Cayce has convinced me at long last that this is an unprofitable operation, less effective even than sticking pins in an effigy. He has brought me to recognize consciously that by working in this negative mode I am doing more harm to myself than to the target of my hostility—plus I waste a lot of valuable time.

With Cayce's advice in mind, I still have to forcibly eject negative thoughts by yanking my mind away from them by sheer force. Gradually this can become a habit, though, restoring time lost in negativity, and it might even bring a better sense of well-being.

Another step Cayce recommends is to look for the better nature in those who irk us. Of course, this is not easy either. There are some people in this world who seem to me to be congenital or self-made jerks; I find it hard to believe they have a good side. On the other hand, they have as much right to be in this world as I do. If I can't change them, I can at least put up with them. And if I can go further and forgive them, this might be the first step in forgiving myself—a practical idea of Cayce's that has struck me as worth a good try.

Question 7: Have you been helped to overcome guilt and fear? If so, how?

According to psychoanalysis, guilt and fear can form the basis of many forms of neurosis. Since the combination of unjustified guilt and fear can mess up a lifetime in short order, I became especially interested in what Edgar Cayce had to say about this. You see, I've found I qualify as a fairly robust neurotic on both these counts; I have the capacity to dredge up guilt feelings even when there is no apparent reason for them.

Cayce's emphasis on avoiding self-condemnation has helped me in this regard. Another helpful premise of Cayce's is that if we recognize our inborn desire to link up with the Creative Force that put us here, and consciously work toward doing that, fears and guilt can be reduced. As I use the tool of meditation in an attempt to attune myself to the universe and to the Creative Force, I am finding a little relief.

Question 8: Has Edgar Cayce helped you find God's will and the nature of free will? If so, how?

The trouble with God's will is that many of us find it hard to place it above our own. I am probably at the front of the line in this regard. Cayce makes it plain that we should put God's will at the top of the priority list at all times. One affirmation Cayce suggests we use to begin a meditation session is emphatic: "Not my will, but *Thine* be done." Forcefully dwelling on this thought has been helpful. Still, we have to face the fact that God has given us our own stubborn and cantankerous will, which continually gets in the way.

Cayce's idea that we firmly align our will with God's can be of great benefit—if we can only get around to doing it. One problem I have is a semantic one: the word "will." It seems sort of threatening at times. We're not supposed to feel threatened by the divine Creative Force that put us here. At least I don't think we are. This is why I have substituted the word "design." For some reason is seems easier to flow with a design than with a will, and to think of God as The Supreme Architect of All Time. Then I can use my own free will as a subcontractor to get to work and help carry out that design. I like to think that God is charitable enough to go along with this idea.

*   *   *

Question 9: Has Edgar Cayce helped you believe in life after death? If so, how?

Edgar Cayce drew a parallel that has helped me considerably with this question. His comparison suggests that death is a rebirth into a new dimension, one that follows the same natural pattern as does our birth into our present earthly existence. Despite the throes of childbirth, despite the many experiences of our earliest years, our progress from total unconsciousness to consciousness is impossible for us to recall. Cayce leads us to believe that we might expect a similar experience upon our demise.

Conceptually, this matches the findings of parapsychologists whose researches have demonstrated considerable evidence that life is continuous, and that some who have died suddenly did not even realize at first that they were dead. Further, Cayce's belief in reincarnation and karma offers encouragement that we can make up for past mistakes and that we can progress toward our ultimate goal.

Question 10: Have you found what religion reveals the greatest truth? If so, what?

Edgar Cayce has helped me understand the difference between religion and spirituality. As I understand it now, religion is a form of worship, while spirituality is an inner quest, a search to achieve "at-onement," to become part of the oneness of God, the Creator, Maker, and First Cause.

It seems, then, that any religion that embraces this totality teaches the importance of following the cosmic laws, and thus is dedicated to the "greatest truth." Cayce subscribes to the "Christ consciousness" as the best path to achieving this. But he does not ignore the value of other great religions and has been careful to avoid dependence on dogma and ritual. Beyond this, he has encouraged us to look within ourselves for a personal God, thereby avoiding the clatter and confusion of religion imposed by authority.

In this way Cayce avoids the tendency of some organized religions to condemn those who sincerely seek the truth in their own way. I have viewed with some dismay the fundamentalists of many faiths who violate other people's rights to seek God freely. Cayce's approach to religion may be "unorthodox" and unique, but in the end I find his focus on the unity of all creation to be consistent with, not in conflict with, belief in the One Supreme God.

THE A.R.E. TODAY

The Association for Research and Enlightenment, Inc. is a non-profit, open membership organization committed to spiritual growth, holistic healing, psychical research and its spiritual dimensions; and more specifically, to making practical use of the psychic readings of the late Edgar Cayce. Through nationwide programs, publications and study groups, A.R.E. offers all those interested, practical information and approaches for individual study groups to better understand and relate to themselves, to other people and to the universe. A.R.E. membership and outreach is concentrated in the United States with growing involvement throughout the world.

The headquarters at Virginia Beach, Virginia include a library/conference center, administrative offices and publishing facilities, and are served by a beachfront motel. The library is one of the largest metaphysical, parapsychological libraries in the country. A.R.E. operates a bookstore, which also offers mail-order service and carries approximately 1,000 titles on nearly every subject related to spiritual growth, world religions, parapsychology and transpersonal psychology. A.R.E. serves its members through nationwide lecture programs, publications, a Braille library, a camp and an extensive Study Group Program.

The A.R.E. facilities, located at 67th Street and Atlantic

Avenue, are open year-round. Visitors are always welcome and may write A.R.E., P.O. Box 595, Virginia Beach, VA 23451, for more informaton about the Association.